THE HUMAN SIDE OF AI

HOW TO THRIVE, ADAPT, AND LEAD WITH HUMANITY IN THE AGE OF INTELLIGENT MACHINES-WHAT EVERY LEADER, PARENT, AND PROFESSIONAL NEEDS TO KNOW ABOUT AI'S HUMAN IMPACT

DR. STEVEN FAIN

CONTENTS

Introduction 5

1. Demystifying AI in Everyday Life 9
2. Building "AI Fluency" Without the Jargon 19
3. Human Strengths in the Age of AI 29
4. Ethical AI for Everyday Decisions 39
5. Adapting Your Career and Skills for the AI Era 49
6. AI and Human Connection 59
7. Digital Well-Being and Mindful Tech Use 69
8. Navigating Bias and Fairness in Everyday AI 78
9. Engaging with AI Policy and Civic Tech 88
10. Global Perspectives and Diverse Voices 98
11. Separating Fact from Fiction 109
12. Taking Action 119

Conclusion 129
References 133

INTRODUCTION

It's morning. You're pouring coffee, scrolling the news, and thinking about your day. You ask your smart speaker to play your favorite song. Your phone suggests a faster route to work. At the office, you get a sales forecast from a tool that knows more about your business than you do. That evening, you help your child with homework, only to wonder if their essay was written by them—or by an algorithm. Maybe later, you will read a story about AI in healthcare, or about someone losing their job to automation. These moments feel normal now. They are woven into daily life. Yet, under the surface, questions and doubts grow.

How do we stay deeply, authentically human—and even thrive—as artificial intelligence becomes part of almost everything we do?

This question keeps me up at night. For over forty years, I have sat with people in my office—parents, workers, leaders, students—helping them face change, loss, and hope. My name is Dr. Steven Fain. I am a clinical psychologist, a speaker, and the author of books that help people adapt and grow. I have seen families navigate digital childhood. I have supported neurodivergent adults who feel both empowered and overwhelmed by technology. I have worked with people who long for connection in a world that feels more distant every year.

Today, I see something new. I see confusion and fear about what AI means for our jobs, privacy, children, and sense of self. People tell me they worry about being replaced at work. They wonder if face-to-face conversation will disappear. They ask, "Can I trust what I see online? Can I trust myself in a world where machines make decisions?" Many want to use AI wisely but are unsure how to start. Others feel frozen by the pace of change. Most of all, I hear a yearning for practical guidance—steps we can take to stay grounded and strong.

You may have noticed that most books about AI fall short. Some are so technical that they lose all but the most devoted experts. Others offer only a gloss, promising simple answers or stoking fear about robots taking over. Many miss what matters most: how AI touches our hearts, changes our relationships, and shapes our vision of a good life. What's missing is a guide that puts people first. That is why I wrote this book.

You hold in your hands a practical, human-centered alternative. Here, you will find frameworks that make sense of AI—not just as technology, but as a force that shapes what it means to live, work, love, and lead. You will read stories of real people—parents, teachers, workers, community leaders—who face these challenges every day. You will discover strategies you can use right away, whether you're learning to talk to your kids about AI or rethinking your own career.

My vision for this book is bold and straightforward. I want to restore the human heartbeat within the age of machines. Progress is powerful only when guided by compassion, wisdom, and purpose. I believe we can build a future where technology serves humanity, not the other way around.

This book is for you if you are curious about AI, whether or not you are technical. It is for educators who want to teach students how to think critically. For parents who wish to prepare their children. For professionals facing work shifts. For community leaders who want to keep people connected. It speaks to a global audience because AI touches every culture, every community, and every home.

Here is what you will find in the pages ahead:

- First, we will explain what AI really is, cutting through hype and jargon.
- Next, we will explore the human strengths that matter most as machines grow smarter—empathy, creativity, resilience, and meaning.
- We will tackle complex questions about ethics, bias, and fairness, and share ways to act with integrity.
- We will look at how work is changing, and how you can adapt your career and skills.
- We will focus on relationships—how to keep them close and real, even as screens and bots multiply.
- We will offer strategies for digital well-being, helping you set boundaries and care for your mind.
- We will examine how AI shapes our communities and democracy, and what it means to be a citizen in a digital world.
- Throughout, we will share myths and truths, stories from around the globe, and practical next steps for your own life.

This book does not promise easy answers. But it does offer hope, clarity, and agency. It is a guide to help you make choices, build habits, and lead with heart—no matter how fast technology moves.

You are not passive in this story. You are not just a user, or a consumer, or a bystander. You are a shaper of what comes next. Together, we can build a future where the best of humanity—our courage, our kindness, our wisdom—grows stronger, not weaker.

The age of AI doesn't have to mean the end of humanity—instead, it can be the beginning of a more mindful, compassionate, and purpose-driven era, if we choose it together.

CHAPTER 1
DEMYSTIFYING AI IN EVERYDAY LIFE

ARTIFICIAL INTELLIGENCE quietly powers much of your daily life, often without you realizing it. Surveys show only a third of people think they use AI, yet over three-quarters actually rely on AI-driven devices or services daily (see Source 1). This perception gap reveals how deeply AI is woven into modern life—no longer the domain of tech companies, but something present in our homes, routines, and even habits. You may interact with AI before leaving your bed, whether through a smart speaker that wakes you with a personalized playlist, a phone that maps your commute before you open the app, or a grocery store app that prompts you for essentials. These are not visions of the future—they are integrated, often unnoticed, parts of daily life.

You may recall when listening to music meant searching through CDs or cooking involved leafing through physical cookbooks. Now, you make a request aloud, and a device not only answers, but personalizes its response. This change crept in over time, often without much thought to how it works or what it means for privacy, habits, and autonomy. This chapter invites you to examine the effects of these invisible helpers, better understand their influence, and become more aware of your own central role in shaping their impact.

RECOGNIZING AI AT HOME—FROM PLAYLISTS TO SMART ASSISTANTS

Start with a familiar example: Spotify's "Discover Weekly." Every Monday, you receive new tracks tailored to your listening history—your likes, skips, and even typical listening times. This system uses "machine learning": it looks for patterns, adapts to your feedback (such as liking or skipping a song), and refines suggestions. The exact process happens when Netflix recommends a show—it bases suggestions on what you watch, how quickly you finish series, and when you pause or stop.

Smart home devices are another place where AI subtly changes routines. Whether you use a voice assistant to set reminders, adjust lighting, or reorder items, each interaction helps the assistant learn your habits—your preferred temperatures, favorite lighting scenes, and even your repeated purchase cycles. Over time, thermostats pre-emptively adjust at bedtime, calendars preload reminders on busy days, and your phone prompts you to restock items like dog food, sometimes before you've thought about it.

This "magic" relies on a feedback loop. Actions like liking a song, dismissing a suggestion, or adjusting settings send signals the AI uses to update its model. Over days and weeks, these signals help customize your experience. Grocery apps, for instance, learn what you buy and how often, and nudge you if you forget staples. These small conveniences streamline life and free mental space for more meaningful activities.

However, convenience comes with tradeoffs—including privacy. AI-enabled devices collect detailed information about your routines, preferences, and sometimes even your voice or location. Many appreciate the time saved, but can feel uneasy when devices accurately anticipate needs without explicit input. The uncanny feeling when a device knows what you need before you say it often points to the vast amount of personal data exchanged for convenience.

Balancing benefits and risks is key. AI tools can free up time and cognitive effort, helping you focus on what truly matters: connections, quiet moments, and creativity. At the same time, they may foster dependency; many now rely on GPS for navigation or smart speakers for reminders that were once handwritten notes.

Try This: Noticing AI in Your Home

Spend a few minutes today tuning in to how AI shapes your routine. Consider:

- Did any device suggest music, news, or entertainment just for you?
- Did you get a personalized reminder from an app?
- Did your grocery app anticipate a need before you remembered?
- Did a device automatically adjust lighting, temperature, or scheduling?

Awareness is the foundation of wise engagement. You don't need to be a technologist to observe these patterns—just be mindful of the small nudges and shortcuts that shape your day. As you become more conscious of AI's influence, you regain the power to choose when and how to let these tools serve what matters most to you.

THE INVISIBLE ALGORITHMS SHAPING YOUR SOCIAL FEEDS

Whenever you scroll through Instagram, Facebook, or Twitter, the content you see is carefully curated by invisible algorithms—complex AI-powered instructions designed to keep you engaged. These platforms aim to have you clicking, watching, and sharing as much as possible. For example, Instagram's Explore page quickly fills with images and videos that reflect your recent searches or likes—check hiking boots once, and your feed fills with outdoor photos and gear reviews. On Facebook, your newsfeed subtly reorganizes itself, showing you more from some friends or groups while others fade away. Even TikTok closely observes each swipe to assemble an addictive, personalized parade of clips you're likely to enjoy.

All these algorithms optimize for engagement. The longer you browse, the more ads you see, and the more data you provide about your preferences. Every like, comment, pause, or skip becomes a valuable clue. YouTube's autoplay, for instance, leads you from one video to the next, quickly turning a short search into an hour-long binge. These platforms are designed to make you lose track of time, with frequent returns for more novelty and amusement.

A related outcome is personalized advertising. This is why you find yourself targeted by ads for shoes right after mentioning sneakers in a chat or briefly searching for something similar online. AI-driven ad systems cross-reference your browsing, engagement history, and even your location to deliver eerily specific promotions. Sometimes this feels helpful; other times, intrusive—almost as if your devices are listening in.

However convenient and entertaining these systems can be, they introduce risks. One primary concern is the "echo chamber" effect. When algorithms prioritize posts and opinions that match your own, you repeatedly see the same kinds of ideas. This "filter bubble" can gradually narrow your perspective, making it harder to encounter new viewpoints or challenge your own. Over time, this shapes not only your online world but also your thinking and mood. Platforms often favor sensational or emotionally charged posts, since these drive higher engagement, which can amplify anxiety or anger in users.

The impact on mood and focus is considerable. Studies suggest algorithm-driven feeds can increase anxiety, foster unhealthy comparisons, and even contribute to loneliness. The constant stream of curated updates can distort reality, making it appear as if everyone else is happier, more successful, or more informed. These platforms are optimized for attention—not for your well-being.

Understanding how these systems work gives you some control. Countless signals drive algorithms: who you interact with, what you pause to watch, which links you open, and even your browsing times. TikTok adapts to each swipe—linger on a gardening video, and you'll see more plant content tomorrow. Every search shapes YouTube recommendations and views to maximize your watch time. These systems aren't inherently malicious—they're engineered to maximize engagement for the company's benefit.

You can, however, reclaim agency over your feed. Deliberately following diverse sources—news, creators from various cultures, differing viewpoints—will introduce more variety. Most platforms also let you label posts as "see less of this" or "not interested." Use these tools often; they help retrain the algorithm better to match your true interests rather than fleeting impulses.

For example, a school counselor I know found her Instagram feed overloaded with stressful posts about education policy, amplifying her anxiety. She strategically followed accounts focusing on art therapy and mindfulness instead. Within weeks, her feed shifted toward lighter, more encouraging topics. She reported feeling calmer and more optimistic as a result.

Ask yourself occasionally: Do my social feeds boost my mood or drag it down? Am I only seeing perspectives I agree with? Am I missing out on discovery? Small actions—hiding posts that trigger anxiety, or seeking out voices different from your own—can help restore balance. Algorithmic curation will always influence your digital experience, but with greater awareness and thoughtful choices, you can make these invisible systems work for you rather than control you.

AI AT WORK—PRACTICAL EXAMPLES IN NON-TECH CAREERS

Step into almost any workplace and you'll find AI quietly influencing the flow of tasks, decisions, and even relationships among colleagues. It's easy to assume that these changes belong to coders or engineers. Still, AI is rapidly becoming a colleague in non-technical sectors, sometimes in ways so seamless you might not even notice. Consider the HR manager who no longer spends days sifting through stacks of resumes. Today, AI-driven screening tools sort candidates, flag potential matches, and even identify patterns in skills or career gaps that a person might miss during a cursory review. These tools use algorithms trained on past hiring data, learning which qualifications align with successful hires and surfacing those applicants for human review. This shift frees HR professionals to focus on interviews, team fit, and onboarding—areas where empathy and instinct matter most. Still, it can create unease, especially when staff wonder whether a missed opportunity was due to an unseen filter or to subtle bias creeping into the algorithm's logic.

In healthcare settings, the presence of AI is also growing. Appointment scheduling systems now analyze patient flow, provider availability, and even historical no-show rates to suggest optimal booking times. Some clinics use AI-driven chatbots to gather preliminary symptoms before a nurse or doctor enters the room. These tools offer efficiency—less time spent on paperwork or chasing down late arrivals—allowing clinicians to invest their energy in what truly matters: patient care. Yet, these benefits come with new kinds of stress. The clinician must trust that the AI isn't missing subtle cues a human might catch. Patients sometimes sense the impersonal nature of digital intake forms, which lack the warmth of a listening ear.

Education is transforming as well. Teachers find themselves using AI-powered grading platforms that analyze student essays for grammar, coherence, and even originality. Adaptive learning platforms track a student's progress in real-time, adjusting questions based on strengths and weaknesses. This technology can give educators more bandwidth to mentor struggling students or design creative lessons. But it also introduces questions about fairness—does the system understand subtle cultural differences in language or learning style? The teacher must now balance trust in the platform's recommendations with professional judgment.

Other roles feel the AI influence in subtler ways. Take a paralegal who once spent hours reviewing lengthy contracts for errors and inconsistencies. Now, AI-driven document analysis scans hundreds of pages in minutes, highlighting red flags for closer inspection. This acceleration means more time for nuanced legal research or client support, but it may also feed "automation anxiety"—the uneasy suspicion that one's expertise could be replaced or undervalued.

Designers experience both inspiration and tension as they adopt generative AI tools for brainstorming logos or layouts. The software produces dozens of options in seconds, sparking new ideas, but the designer must guard against losing their distinctive voice. Originality remains crucial; clients still expect work that feels human, not algorithmic.

Even beyond creative and professional roles, AI quietly shapes routine office life. Small business owners rely on dashboards that generate sales forecasts using historical data and seasonal trends. These predictions inform inventory purchases or marketing campaigns—decisions once based on gut feeling, now steered by data patterns most people could never spot on their own. Email platforms like Outlook or Gmail use AI to automatically sort messages by priority, flagging urgent requests and filtering out distractions. Many professionals accept this as background noise until they miss an essential message filtered away by an unseen rule.

In each sector, the same pattern emerges: AI streamlines repetitive work, surfaces trends invisible to the naked eye, and opens space for more meaningful engagement with colleagues and customers. However, these benefits rarely arrive without challenges—uncertainty about transparency, the fear of deskilling, and concerns about bias woven into every decision an algorithm makes.

Reflection Exercise: Mapping AI in Your Workday

Spend a day observing your work tasks. Use this checklist to notice where AI might play a hand:

- Did you use software that recommends next steps or flags urgent emails?
- Was any part of your workflow—grading, scheduling, client communication—automated or "assisted" by a tool?
- Did you interact with dashboards offering predictions or analysis?
- Did you notice automated suggestions for design, writing, or planning?
- Were hiring decisions or candidate reviews filtered by an algorithm?

Circle each touchpoint you recognize. Reflect on which aspects feel supportive and which raise questions for you about transparency or fairness. Awareness is the first step toward thoughtful engagement with these new tools—keeping your role meaningful even as automation grows around you.

A Day in the Life—Personal AI Diaries from Real People

Morning in Singapore, a teacher prepares for class behind her laptop. The quiet time before students arrive is valuable for planning. She uses an AI lesson planner that suggests activities based on her students' recent progress—who needs help with fractions, who's ready for a creative task. The tool often picks up on trends she might miss during a busy week. She hesitates when shown a lesson format she's never used, but decides to try it, curious about the outcome. Mid-morning, she's rewarded when a struggling student finally understands a topic, but she wonders if she's giving up too much control. While technology saves her hours, she sometimes misses the joy of crafting each lesson herself.

In Toronto, midday brings multitasking for a parent juggling work emails and lunch. Their phone pings—a reminder from a virtual assistant about an upcoming school meeting, plus a dinner recipe based on what's in the fridge. This personalized support makes life smoother, almost magical. However, an alert about a new after-school program pauses them. Did they say something about this, or search for it? The system's awareness feels both helpful and intrusive, leaving them grateful yet uneasy.

In London, early afternoon finds a community organizer striving to boost turnout for an event. She checks her analytics—her posts are reaching fewer people, likely due to another algorithm change. She tests new hashtags and formats, adapting to the platform's invisible rules. It's frustrating to chase engagement, knowing her efforts depend on opaque systems. Still, previous insights from analytics have expanded her message's reach, making her grateful for data-driven advice even as she struggles to stay true to her mission.

In rural America, evening falls as an artist sits with her tablet and stylus, prompting an AI image generator with ideas inspired by the local landscape. Instantly, vibrant digital paintings appear—familiar fields transformed with surprising hues and forms. Some creations spark new ideas for her traditional canvas work. Collaboration with AI excites her, but raises questions about authenticity: Is it still her art if the process feels shared? She's inspired but anxious that her own creative touch might become less recognizable or valued.

Back in Singapore, a retiree winds down with a cup of tea, reviewing health data from his wearable device. The app notices minor changes in his heart rate and sleep and softly recommends a doctor's check-in. This gentle nudge reassures him, as if someone is keeping a watchful eye on his well-being. Yet, he sometimes worries he's relying too much on these alerts. What if something gets missed? The sense of security is real, but so is the vulnerability of trusting technology with what once seemed personal.

These stories illustrate AI as both helper and puzzle—a presence that brings comfort, confusion, and sometimes anxiety. One person applauds an app's precision; another feels unsettled by its intrusive insights. These aren't just isolated anecdotes—they show how deeply technology now integrates with daily life around the globe.

The experiences reveal the paradoxes of living with AI: efficiency but less control, surprise but hints of suspicion, and innovation at the cost of traditions. The impact varies widely—by context, culture, age, and job. Teachers may feel empowered or challenged by innovative tools; artists gain inspiration but question their role; parents balance convenience with privacy; organizers seek fairness in digital spaces; retirees weigh safety against autonomy.

Reflective Prompt: Your Own AI Touchpoints

Pause and reflect on your own day. Where did AI intersect with your choices or routines—big or small? Over the next 24 hours, jot down each instance. How did these moments feel: comforting, surprising, uneasy, empowering? Awareness is a first step to truly understanding how these technologies shape our daily lives.

No one—myself included—has all the answers, but by observing and discussing each encounter, we become more mindful and intentional with these invisible companions by our side, from morning to night.

CHAPTER 2
BUILDING "AI FLUENCY" WITHOUT THE JARGON

EXPLAINING AI TO A FRIEND—USING EVERYDAY ANALOGIES

IMAGINE you are sitting across from a friend at a coffee shop, both of you glancing at your phones as you wait for your drinks. Your friend asks, "What exactly is AI, anyway?" In this moment, the best answer is not a list of technical terms, but a story or analogy that makes sense in the real world. Think about a child learning to tell the difference between dogs and cats. You show her dozens of pictures—some with floppy ears, some with pointy faces. At first, she might get confused, calling a fox a dog, or a lion a cat. But gradually, with each example and gentle correction, she starts to spot the patterns. She notices the shape of the ears, the length of the tail, and soon, she can tell a beagle from a tabby without much help. When you describe AI "learning," picture this: Instead of a child, it's a computer looking at thousands of images. With each picture, the AI receives feedback—right or wrong—until it becomes better at making those same distinctions. It's not magic, nor is it an accurate understanding. It's repetition, pattern recognition, and correction, just like a child with a picture book.

Now, think about AI as a chef following a recipe. Imagine a cook who has never tasted chocolate cake. She receives dozens of recipes, some with more sugar, others with extra cocoa. After baking and tasting each cake, she begins to predict which combinations will lead to the most decadent flavor. She tweaks the recipe, learns from mistakes, and gradually, her cakes improve. AI works like this, chef: It experiments, predicts outcomes, tests results, and refines the "recipe" over time. When you ask your voice assistant for a dinner suggestion, it is drawing from its vast cookbook—recipes shaped by millions of user preferences and feedback.

You might find yourself trying to explain this at a family dinner or during a book club discussion. Here's a simple way to describe "training data." Picture yourself teaching your dog to sit. Each time she sits, you reward her with a treat; when she gets it wrong, you withhold the treat but offer encouragement. Over time, the dog learns what earns rewards. AI systems "learn" in a similar way, except their treats are correct answers and their lessons come from thousands—or even millions—of examples. When you want to explain "neural networks," use the idea of a group of people in a room, each with a slightly different opinion about the answer to a question. They talk, share ideas, and eventually reach a consensus through discussion. That's how neural networks function: Each part offers input, and through many rounds of "voting," they settle on an answer that reflects the group's shared wisdom.

Stories and metaphors do more than simplify; they build connection and foster accurate understanding. I remember a parent explaining AI to her child by using Lego blocks. She said, "Imagine each block is a tiny piece of information. Alone, one block doesn't do much. But when you put them together in the right way, they form something new—a castle, a spaceship, a whole world. AI is like building with Legos, using many pieces to create answers and solve problems." The child's eyes lit up—the idea clicked because it was built on something familiar and concrete. This approach works because it anchors new ideas to lived experience, making abstract concepts accessible and memorable.

When you practice explaining AI in this way, you also empower yourself. You become not just a learner, but a translator—a bridge between the technical and the everyday. This is especially powerful in group settings, like work meetings where colleagues may feel intimidated by tech jargon, or at community gatherings where skepticism reigns. You might say, "Think of AI like a recipe that improves each time someone tastes the dish and gives feedback. Or like a team brainstorming solutions until they agree on the best path forward." These metaphors invite curiosity, lower defenses, and encourage questions—transforming confusion into dialogue.

Practice Exercise: Explaining AI in Your Own Words

Pick someone in your life—a partner, friend, or coworker. Choose one AI concept (like machine learning or neural networks) and explain it using an analogy drawn from daily life, such as cooking, sports, or hobbies. Notice their reaction—did your story help them "see" the idea more clearly? Jot down what worked and where you stumbled. Over time, refine your analogies based on real conversations. This is how you build your own fluency and confidence, one story at a time.

DECODING AI BUZZWORDS—A PRACTICAL GLOSSARY

Headlines and conversations about artificial intelligence are filled with jargon that can seem confusing. If talk of algorithms and neural networks leaves you lost, you're not alone. To understand AI, it helps to break down these terms and relate them to everyday life.

An "algorithm" is simply a set of instructions—a step-by-step recipe for computers. For example, Spotify uses algorithms to create personalized playlists by analyzing what you've listened to and suggesting new songs based on those patterns.

"Machine learning" happens when computers improve at tasks by learning from data, rather than following fixed rules. Consider your email's spam filter that becomes better at blocking unwanted messages as you continue to mark spam; it adapts and learns from your choices. "Deep learning" is a more advanced form, inspired by how the human brain works. Imagine it as layered processes: one finds edges in photos, another detects shapes, and together they recognize faces.

"Training data" refers to the examples an AI system reviews before making predictions. It's like a chef perfecting a dish after tasting many versions. In AI, this could be thousands of labeled photos (cat or dog) or millions of sentences used to teach a language model grammar and writing style.

A "model" is the trained AI itself—the part that makes predictions or generates responses. This is what's at work when you use autocomplete or talk to a virtual assistant; like a chef who's mastered a recipe, the model confidently produces results you interact with.

"Bias" occurs when AI systems show unfounded preferences, often reflecting imbalances in the data they learned from. For instance, if a hiring app favors resumes from certain schools or with particular names, that's bias—shaping outcomes quietly until someone investigates.

"Automation" is when machines or software take over tasks, such as autopay for bills or self-checkout at stores. With AI, automation can tackle more complex tasks, such as reviewing legal documents for errors or creating personalized news summaries.

A "black box" is an AI system whose decision-making process is unclear—even to its designers. For instance, you might not know why your loan is denied or why your online feed looks a certain way; the reasoning remains hidden, raising concerns about transparency.

"Natural language processing" (NLP) enables computers to understand and respond to human language. Features like phone autocorrect, voice assistants, and translation tools rely on NLP to convert digital information into forms that humans can easily use —conversations or text.

"GPT" stands for Generative Pre-trained Transformer, a popular type of large language model. This technology, found in tools like ChatGPT, reads vast amounts of text to learn how humans write and uses that knowledge to generate responses to questions.

"Augmented intelligence" highlights how AI boosts, rather than replaces, human ability. For example, doctors may use AI to help scan X-rays, but they still apply their medical expertise—just with added, data-driven insight.

"Human-in-the-loop" means people remain involved in AI decisions rather than letting the system act entirely on its own. For example, a bank's AI may flag a suspicious transaction, but a human reviews it before any action is taken.

Beware of words like "revolutionary," "autonomous," "disruptive," and "sentient" in marketing and headlines. "Revolutionary" claims deserve scrutiny—does the tool really change things, or is it hype? Most "autonomous" systems still require human oversight. "Disruptive" suggests instant, massive change, but fundamental transformation is gradual. "Sentient" implies self-awareness, which AI does not possess, no matter how the media portrays it.

Test Yourself: AI Buzzwords in Action

Fill in the blanks using terms from above:

1. The system that organizes your news feed by tracking what you click is called an ______________.
2. When your phone corrects your spelling as you type, it uses ______________.
3. If an AI tool unfairly prefers certain job applicants, this is known as ______________.
4. A self-checkout lane in a store is an example of ______________.
5. The term for AI that needs human oversight for key decisions is ______________.

Check your answers: 1) algorithm, 2) natural language processing, 3) bias, 4) automation, 5) human-in-the-loop.

SPOTTING HYPE VS. REALITY IN THE NEWS

Artificial intelligence rarely leaves the headlines these days. Almost every week, a new article or press release makes bold promises—or dire warnings—about what AI can or will do. For you, the reader, it can feel impossible to know what's real, what's exaggerated, and what's just clickbait. The stories often blend fact and fiction so smoothly that sorting them apart requires a careful, skeptical eye. When reading about AI, begin by asking a straightforward question: Is this claim grounded in real evidence, or is it mostly someone's opinion or an attempt to stir up excitement? If a story says, "AI will replace all jobs," pause and look for concrete data. Who collected the numbers? What kinds of jobs are they talking about? Does the article mention specific changes already happening, or does it rely on vague predictions about the distant future? Sweeping statements often hide more than they reveal.

Another thing to watch for is confusion between narrow AI—programs that perform specific tasks, like sorting photos or recommending movies—and general AI, which refers to machines with intelligence like a human's, able to understand, reason, and adapt to new situations on their own. Most current news about AI actually describes narrow systems, yet headlines sometimes blur this line. If you see claims that "scientists have built an AI that feels emotions," ask yourself, are they talking about a chatbot that mimics feelings, or something truly self-aware? Usually, it's the first. Language like "AI passes the Turing Test" often means a program fooled some people in a limited conversation, not that it gained consciousness or human understanding. This distinction matters because it shapes how we respond—practically and emotionally—to new technology.

Red flags in AI news show up in headlines that promise either utopia or disaster. "AI will take over democracy!" "AI writes award-winning novels from scratch!" These stories thrive on sensationalism, but rarely deliver on their claims. Job replacement stories make good headlines but seldom acknowledge that many roles change, not vanish. Often, the same technology that automates one task creates a demand for new skills elsewhere. Beware stories that present change as one-sided or straightforward. Likewise, when an article describes a machine with feelings or creativity, read carefully. Is the system truly generating something new, or is it rearranging old ideas in a novel way? Human creativity involves experience, context, and emotion—elements that current AI systems do not possess.

One way to build your news literacy is to compare coverage from different sources. If you see a viral AI claim, look for follow-up reporting in publications such as Wired, MIT Technology Review, The Guardian, or Al Jazeera. These outlets tend to provide depth and balance, often including voices from skeptics as well as advocates. They ask more complex questions about ethics, bias, and real-world impact, rather than repeating a company's press release or chasing clicks. When several reputable publications cover a topic in similar detail, you can usually trust there's substance behind the headline. If only one site is shouting about a breakthrough, caution is wise.

As you work to separate signal from noise in AI news, keep a checklist in mind: Is the article clear about what the AI system actually does? Does it confuse narrow and general intelligence? Are there specific examples, or only sweeping statements? Are counterarguments or expert doubts included? If the story relies on dramatic language—"revolutionary," "sentient," "autonomous genius"—step back and look for calmer, more nuanced analysis elsewhere.

Myth-Busting Sidebar: Recent AI Headlines

- "AI Passes the Turing Test!"
The reality: In one limited setting, a chatbot convinced some people it was human during a short online conversation. This does not mean the program understands, feels, or reasons like a person. It mimics conversation patterns without proper comprehension.

- "AI Writes Novels from Scratch!"
The reality: AI programs can generate long texts by predicting likely words and phrases based on their training data. Some passages may be impressive, but the stories lack deep characterization and emotional nuance. Human editors often rewrite or guide the output to create readable work.

- "AI Will Take Over Democracy!"
The reality: Some AI-driven tools influence public opinion by shaping social media feeds or targeting ads. However, the idea

that AI will seize control of democratic processes is exaggerated. Human decisions, laws, and oversight remain central to elections and governance.

Whenever you come across headlines like these, slow down and look for what's missing. Ask whether the system is honestly thinking or simply following patterns. Seek out experts who highlight both benefits and risks. Healthy skepticism isn't cynicism—it's your best tool for making sense of a fast-changing world where hype often outpaces reality.

THE "BLACK BOX" PROBLEM—MAKING SENSE OF OPAQUE AI DECISIONS

People love tools that work—a coffee maker, a face-unlocking phone, a spot-on weather app. But with artificial intelligence, these "magic" moments mask a deeper issue: the black-box problem. Imagine a blender so complicated that even its engineers can't explain how it works. You get a smoothie, but what happens inside remains a mystery. That's the essence of many AI systems: they pull in data, produce results, but their internal reasoning is tangled and largely invisible.

This lack of transparency isn't a mere technical quirk—it can become a serious issue when AI influences real lives. Consider a loan applicant rejected by an algorithm, with only a form letter for explanation and no one able to say why the decision was made. Or in healthcare, where doctors may receive AI-generated treatment advice that feels wrong, yet even the developers can offer little rationale beyond "that's what the system determined." The same opacity affects hiring: software filters applicants and spits out rankings, often without a clear explanation. In all these scenarios, people are left powerless, struggling to trust decisions they can't review or question—especially when essential stakes are involved.

Mistakes from these systems can have serious consequences. There are numerous examples of AI-driven decisions unjustly denying mortgages, misdiagnosing patients, or selecting unqualified job candidates. Often, the data used to train AI carries unexamined biases or errors from the past. Even if a system appears objective, its decisions may reflect old prejudices or simple inaccuracies. When something goes wrong, accountability is elusive—can rejected applicants appeal? Is there any clear explanation for the outcome, or is it buried in the algorithm's workings? This breeds distrust and risk, particularly for those already facing discrimination.

When dealing with a black-box system—whether at work, at the doctor's, or as a customer—adopt a questioning mindset. Who is responsible for decisions? Is there any human oversight, or is it all left to the algorithm? Insist on clear explanations of how decisions are made and what data is used. In organizations, advocate for policies to handle AI-driven choices: What is the recourse for someone denied an opportunity by an AI? Who ensures accuracy, fairness, and checks for bias? If explanations are lacking, do not simply accept "that's just how it works." Demand transparency.

You can also take practical steps to protect yourself. If an AI system decides for you, request an explanation in plain language. For example, you might write:

"Hello, I recently received a decision from your automated system regarding [loan application, job interview, etc.]. I would appreciate a clear explanation of how this decision was reached and who is responsible for reviewing these outcomes. Can you provide information on how I may appeal or request human review?"

Beyond individual action, raise awareness in your workplace or community. Suggest that your organization use a checklist before implementing any AI tool:

Five Questions to Ask Before Trusting an AI System:

1. Who is accountable for the system's decisions?
2. Can outcomes be explained clearly?
3. Is there an appeals process for mistakes or unfair results?
4. How is the data used screened for bias and errors?

5. Are multiple, diverse perspectives involved in developing and reviewing the system?

For instance, one employee at a mid-sized company noticed that a new hiring AI consistently overlooked qualified candidates from specific backgrounds. Instead of staying silent, she documented her concerns and brought them to HR. Her particular questions led to a review and the addition of a human reviewer for flagged resumes, improving fairness and rebuilding staff trust in the process.

The black box problem isn't going away. As AI grows more powerful and common, the need for transparency and accountability expands with it. By asking questions, demanding clarity, and sharing your experiences, you pressure organizations to create better, fairer systems—and remind them that technology must serve people, not the other way around.

As you finish this chapter, remember: opaque AI may feel intimidating, but you are not helpless. With the right questions and persistent advocacy, you can bring light to even the most complex systems. Next, we'll examine uniquely human strengths—like creativity and empathy—that no algorithm can replicate. These are the traits that will help you succeed, regardless of technology's future.

CHAPTER 3
HUMAN STRENGTHS IN THE AGE OF AI

CREATIVITY UNPLUGGED—USING AI AS A MUSE, NOT A REPLACEMENT

IMAGINE YOURSELF IN A SUNLIT STUDIO, a blank canvas before you, and a palette of colors at hand. There's an anticipation—the spark when a new idea flits at the edge of awareness. Now picture an unseen partner: one that never tires, always offers new suggestions, but cannot dream. This is how AI fits into creativity today—not as the artist, but as a tireless muse nudging you in novel directions. AI is like a mood board, curating unexpected images, sounds, or phrases. A designer, for instance, uploads sketches into an AI program and, within seconds, receives an array of mood boards. Some elements are familiar, others unexpected. The AI doesn't judge or edit; it simply recombines existing patterns. The designer feels surprise and control, picking what resonates. Her creativity isn't replaced—it's reignited.

Writers, too, experience this blend of inspiration and autonomy. An AI text generator can help break writer's block by proposing outlines, posing questions, or suggesting fresh turns of phrase. Yet, the lines that matter most—the ones with rhythm and meaning—are still distinctly human. One novelist I know uses GPT tools to plot complex stories, letting the machine suggest possibilities around setting or character conflict. After a basic outline appears, she writes the dialogue and emotions, shaping the work into her unique voice. Here, AI is just a brainstorming partner—fast and tireless, but never truly original.

There's a clear difference between machine-produced content and authentic human creation. Poems or stories by AI may sound polished, even clever, but they lack soul. Their words echo what's already out there; they don't reveal lived experience or vulnerability. A poet may edit algorithm-suggested lines, shaping each verse until it fits her cadence and emotion. Creativity comes alive at the points where intuition diverges from machine logic—where you keep a flaw, take a leap, or invent something no software would suggest. This authenticity—your creative fingerprint—matters now more than ever.

Working with AI means being both open and selective. The "Yes, and…" improv technique can help: accept an AI suggestion, then build on it in your own style. If an AI proposes a strange color palette, instead of dismissing it, you might ask, "What if I use these to evoke a mood, or blend them with my favorites?" The goal isn't to surrender to the machine but to let surprise drive you. Set clear boundaries for AI input; trust your instincts and shape suggestions until they feel right.

Interactive Element: Your Creative Voice Checklist

- Do I feel engaged or detached using AI for inspiration?
- Can I clearly identify which parts of my work are mine?
- Am I keeping quirks and ideas AI would never suggest?
- When do I trust my intuition over algorithmic advice?
- Have I experimented with remixing or reinterpreting AI suggestions?

Reflect on these after each session. Patterns will appear: times when AI sparks genuine curiosity, and when it distracts from your instincts.

Across professions and around the world, people are blending their talents with AI in striking ways. A jazz musician might start with an AI-generated beat, then improvise live melodies over it. The algorithm is only a launch pad; each solo has his own. An entrepreneur reviews

AI analytics to spot surprising trends. Instead of just following the data, she lets those patterns inspire product ideas rooted in empathy—needs she grasps from experience. Artists use image generators for fresh forms and textures, later refining those drafts into statements by hand.

These examples show that creativity thrives in dialogue—with tools, communities, and even algorithms. But you remain the author of meaning. Machines can suggest patterns and possibilities, but they cannot feel wonder or improvise in the moment. Engage with AI as a collaborator, not a rival. This way, creativity stays fully human—surprising, imperfect, and alive.

THE EMPATHY GAP—MAINTAINING EMOTIONAL INTELLIGENCE IN DIGITAL SPACES

Digital and AI-mediated communication has changed how we relate to one another, sometimes leaving us feeling more alone even as we are more connected than ever. The "empathy gap" refers to the distance created when technology becomes a filter for human emotion—a barrier that can lead to misunderstandings, disconnection, or even unintended hurt. When interactions move from face-to-face to screens, subtle cues vanish. You can't see a colleague's nervous smile in an email, or sense a friend's hesitation through a chatbot. Even the best AI cannot read the tension in a room or the warmth in a voice. This gap grows wider when organizations automate sensitive tasks. Imagine a manager who once delivered feedback in person but now relies on automated performance reviews. Team members may feel unseen, their struggles reduced to metrics and scores. The result is often a steady decline in morale, which numbers alone can't explain.

Emotional intelligence—the ability to recognize, understand, and respond to emotions, both your own and others'—becomes more vital in these digital spaces. The challenge is to restore feeling and nuance where algorithms flatten everything into data points. One of the most effective ways to do this is through "active listening," especially in virtual meetings. This means silencing notifications, making eye contact with your camera, and reflecting on what you hear. Simple phrases like "It sounds like you're frustrated," or "I notice you paused—do you want to say more?" bridge the gap that screens create. Personal touches matter, too. Instead of defaulting to AI-generated emails, send a short voice note. The sound of an authentic voice—its pauses, inflections, and stumbles—carries empathy that text alone cannot deliver. It signals presence, effort, and care.

In tech-heavy environments, staying emotionally attuned to yourself is just as important as staying connected to others. Digital overload and rapid-fire communication can numb your senses, making it easy to react rather than respond. Building in moments for self-reflection can act as an anchor. Daily gratitude journaling, even if it's just three sentences scribbled in a notebook or on your phone, draws your attention to what feels meaningful or joyful. Gratitude shifts your mind toward connection and abundance. Another helpful tool is the "three-minute mindful pause" before responding to digital messages. Sit back, close your eyes, and notice your breath. Ask yourself, "What am I feeling?" and "What does this person need right now?" This practice interrupts the impulse to reply on autopilot, allowing empathy to guide your next step.

Some organizations are getting creative about building empathy in digital-first workplaces. I've seen teachers hold virtual "wellness check-ins" with students, asking how they're feeling using a simple color code or a quick open-ended question. These check-ins foster trust and give young people language for their emotions, even at a distance. Customer service teams are also experimenting with blending chatbot efficiency and human warmth. A bot might answer initial queries, but more complex or emotional issues get routed to a live agent trained to listen and resolve concerns with patience and understanding. This layered approach respects both speed and sensitivity.

Self-awareness is the foundation for bridging the empathy gap. Technology tempts us to move fast and multitask, but emotional connection requires presence. If you notice irritability or distance creeping into your digital exchanges, pause and recalibrate. Consider setting reminders to check in with yourself throughout the day. Ask: "Am I truly present for this interaction? Have I acknowledged the other person's feelings, not just their words?" Over time, these habits become part of your digital routine, infusing even the most mundane exchanges with humanity.

Prompts and tools can help you stay grounded. Try placing a sticky note on your screen with a single word: "Listen." Or set a calendar alert titled "Check empathy" before team meetings. In moments of conflict or confusion, step away from the keyboard and give yourself space before replying. It's remarkable how a few deep breaths and a moment of reflection can shift your response from reactive to compassionate. In organizations that prioritize empathy, you'll notice higher morale, loyalty, and even productivity. People are more willing to share ideas, admit mistakes, and support each other when they feel seen and heard —not just measured or managed.

Stories abound of workplaces making empathy a priority, even—and especially—when distance threatens to erode it. One school principal I know schedules fifteen minutes each week for virtual "coffee chats" with staff, focusing on personal connection rather than performance. After introducing this routine, teachers reported feeling less isolated and more valued. In the customer service world, some companies now send handwritten notes to clients after a difficult call—a simple gesture that stands out in a sea of automated replies. These acts remind us that technology is only as compassionate as the people who use it. Your ability to maintain emotional intelligence in digital spaces will not only strengthen your relationships but also set a tone for those around you —one where empathy, not automation, guides the way forward.

CRITICAL THINKING IN AN ALGORITHMIC WORLD

You live in a time when digital assistants offer instant answers, curated headlines flood your phone, and AI-driven recommendations quietly shape what you see, buy, or believe. Yet even as algorithms promise ease, your ability to pause, question, and analyze grows more urgent. Critical thinking—questioning, verifying, and contextualizing—

remains a deeply human strength. The world has always needed skeptics, but today, your skepticism is a shield not only against misinformation but also against the subtle influence of machine logic. Imagine a social media user watching a news story gain traction overnight. Instead of sharing it on impulse, she pauses and asks, "Who posted this? Is it credible? What's missing?" This pause is not just wise; it's powerful.

You will encounter AI-generated outputs every day, from product suggestions to health advice, and even financial predictions. Each result carries the risk of error, bias, or shallow reasoning—risks multiplied by the speed and scope of machine processing. Blind trust is a temptation, but it erodes your agency. Instead, equip yourself with frameworks designed for scrutiny. The SIFT method—Stop, Investigate the source, Find better coverage, Trace claims—offers a simple, practical way to dissect online content. Begin by stopping. Take a breath before clicking or sharing. Next, investigate the source. Does it have a history of accuracy? Look for coverage from other sources; reputable outlets will corroborate or challenge the information. Finally, trace claims back to their roots. Is that viral statistic really from a peer-reviewed study, or just a blog post with a convincing headline? This method, though straightforward, gives you leverage over the flood of AI-shaped content.

Relying on a single algorithm, platform, or tool creates echo chambers and blind spots. You strengthen your judgment by comparing outputs across tools and with human experts. Suppose you receive health advice from a popular AI chatbot. Does it align with your doctor's recommendations? If two AI platforms deliver conflicting investment predictions, which aligns with independent market data or trusted advisors? This cross-verification is not tedious; it's protective. It transforms you from consumer to evaluator—someone who shapes their own understanding rather than absorbing whatever comes first or loudest.

Practice is key. Consider a professional who receives two business reports, both generated by different AI analytics suites. Each report paints a distinct picture of next quarter's forecast. Instead of picking the more optimistic analysis, she checks the data sources, notes assumptions, and asks human colleagues for their take. The act of comparison reveals gaps: one report uses outdated data, the other makes bold predictions based on volatile trends. The professional blends these findings with her own domain knowledge, crafting a strategy that balances machine insight with lived experience. In another scenario, a parent reviews educational content recommended by an adaptive learning app. The app claims to tailor lessons perfectly to the child's needs, but the parent notices some exercises feel repetitive or out of sync with schoolwork. Rather than simply trusting the app, she asks teachers for feedback, tries alternative resources, and closely watches her child's engagement. This mix of vigilance and curiosity protects against over-reliance and keeps learning meaningful.

Thought experiments offer another way to hone critical thinking. Picture yourself as a manager evaluating an AI-based hiring tool that claims to remove bias. Would you accept its shortlist at face value? What questions would you ask about how it scores candidates? Imagine you're a consumer comparing AI-generated reviews about a new medication. Would you trust glowing summaries if you can't find any clinical evidence? These exercises cultivate habits that become second nature—habits of pressing for details, seeking context, and weighing consequences.

Machines excel at pattern recognition, but they cannot grasp nuance or context the way you can. Algorithms work with data from the past; humans imagine futures and consider ethics, outliers, and human cost. Your challenge is not to reject AI outright, but to remain an active participant in every exchange. When you spot inconsistencies or signs of manipulation—a quote out of context, a suspiciously perfect review, a chain of "facts" with no source—trust your instincts and investigate further.

You might notice, too, that critical thinking is contagious. When you model skepticism in meetings, family discussions, or online forums, others feel empowered to do the same. Over time, this collective vigilance raises the standard for truth and trust in your circles, both digital and real. The reward is not just better decisions, but greater confidence in your own mind and in the integrity of your community.

NURTURING MORAL JUDGMENT—WHEN AI CAN'T MAKE THE CALL

Machines can compute probabilities, sort through massive datasets, and even mimic patterns of ethical reasoning, but they do not feel the weight of justice or compassion. When it comes to ethics and fairness, AI systems have absolute limits—boundaries that no amount of data can cross. These systems absorb the patterns and biases present in their training material, which means that, left unchecked, they often repeat past injustices rather than correct them. In hiring, for example, algorithms sort candidates by parsing résumés and searching for keywords. If the historical data behind the system reflects bias—favoring specific names, schools, or work histories—those patterns get reinforced rather than questioned. The result? Qualified people may never get a fair look, and a company's culture can quietly stagnate. No algorithm, no matter how advanced, can replace the nuanced judgment and lived experience that people bring to questions of fairness and equity.

Now and then, the consequences of relying on AI become painfully clear. Imagine a hospital using a machine-learning model to recommend cancer treatments. The algorithm suggests an aggressive plan, citing statistics and survival rates. Yet the physician, recognizing the patient's age, values, and the impact on family, pauses. She takes into account not just what the data suggests, but who the patient is—a parent, a teacher, someone who treasures quality of life over a few extra months. She discusses options, listens, and guides the decision alongside the person affected. The algorithm is practical, but it is not the final authority. In schools, similar dilemmas arise. AI may flag students as "at-risk" using attendance records, test scores, or behavioral data. But a counselor sees beyond the numbers, understanding that a flagged student might just be coping with a parent's illness or a temporary housing crisis. Instead of treating the child as a data point, the counselor advocates for extra support and connection, not just intervention. Here, the human touch brings dignity and possibility—something no program can replicate.

To act wisely in these moments, you need practical tools for reflection. One approach is the "Ethical Pause"—a deliberate moment to ask three vital questions before acting on AI advice: Does this decision respect the dignity of those affected? Is it fair to all involved, especially the most vulnerable? What would I do if my actions were made public? This brief check-in slows the process, creating space for values to guide your choices rather than efficiency or convenience. Another helpful method is the "Four Lenses" model. Before accepting any automated recommendation, consider: How does this impact the individual? What are the consequences for the broader community? Do cultural norms or histories shape what's at stake? And what are the long-term effects, including risks or harms that may not be visible right away? By looking through these lenses in turn, you shift from a quick technical answer to a thoughtful, human-centered decision.

Examples of people stepping up for human values are everywhere if you look. A human resources team at a midsize company discovered that its recruitment software consistently overlooked candidates from specific backgrounds. Instead of ignoring the pattern, they paused the use of the tool, brought in outside experts to review its logic, and returned to manual screening until they could guarantee fairness. They faced pushback about productivity and cost, but decided that inclusion mattered more than speed. In another city, a council member noticed that AI-powered policing software was being used to predict crime "hotspots," raising concerns about privacy and racial profiling. She called for public hearings, demanded algorithmic transparency, and insisted on community oversight. Her efforts led to policy changes—and a broader conversation about the kind of society the city wanted to build.

These stories remind us that while AI can process more data than any individual, only people can weigh meaning, context, and conscience. Technology should support ethical decision-making, not override it. When you sense discomfort with an automated recommendation, listen to that voice. Pause, reflect, and ask questions that push beyond convenience. True fairness means staying engaged, even when it's difficult or unpopular.

As this chapter closes, remember: your moral judgment brings light where algorithms can't reach. The next chapter will focus on adapting your skills and career so you continue to thrive in a world shaped by AI—always keeping humanity at the center of progress.

CHAPTER 4
ETHICAL AI FOR EVERYDAY DECISIONS

THE HUMAN-CENTRIC AI CHECKLIST—A STEP-BY-STEP GUIDE

EVERY DAY, we encounter moments when artificial intelligence shapes our choices, whether at home, at work, or in our communities. It's no longer about whether you'll interact with AI, but about deciding which tools you can trust and how those choices reflect your values.

To help navigate this, use a practical, human-centered AI checklist—a set of guiding questions for evaluating any AI tool before using it. This list is meant for real, complex situations, and it respects that your time is limited.

First, consider: "Is this AI tool transparent about its decisions?" Transparency means you can find clear, understandable explanations about what the tool does, how it makes decisions, and who is accountable if something goes wrong. For example, if you have an AI thermostat, the company should explain how it learns your preferences and what data it uses. Similarly, if your workplace implements an AI résumé screener, ask for detailed yet straightforward information on how applicants are filtered and which data is used. A transparent system avoids jargon and provides explanations anyone can understand.

Next, ask about recourse: "Is there a way to contest or appeal decisions made by this tool?" For instance, if your child's school uses an AI to flag students as "at risk" but provides no explanation, a sound system would allow you to ask questions or request a human review. In the workplace, if an AI scheduling tool assigns you impossible shifts, you should be able to dispute those choices. Recourse ensures fairness, keeping technology in the service of people, not the other way around.

Third, address bias: "Does this AI challenge or reinforce unfair patterns?" AI systems learn from data that can contain social biases, which the AI may then amplify. For example, a hiring AI trained mostly on male résumés might undervalue female applicants—something that has happened in practice. At home, a voice assistant that struggles with certain accents can exclude users. In the community, predictive policing tools have sometimes unfairly targeted specific neighborhoods. It's essential to check if the developers have examined and sought to reduce such biases. If not, seek out answers or consider a different tool.

Personalize the checklist based on your needs. An educator might ask whether a learning app supports different learning styles; a healthcare worker might focus on patient safety and ask whether reliable sources back recommendations. Parents may concentrate on privacy, wondering whether an AI respects their family's data and allows them to control who sees it. Ask yourself: "For my role as a ___________, the most important ethical feature is __________." This reflection helps you align your choices with your values.

A practical example: Your company is piloting an AI résumé screener, and you're on the hiring team. Begin with transparency: Request documentation on how the AI ranks candidates and what data it uses. See if the company can explain its decisions to rejected applicants. For recourse, ensure that candidates can escalate questionable choices to a human reviewer. With bias, ask whether the tool was tested for discrimination (e.g., against certain schools or people with employment gaps). If responses are vague, recommend a test period in which human and AI choices are compared for potential unfair patterns, making adjustments as necessary.

Interactive Element: Personalize Your AI Checklist

Try creating your personal version of the Human-Centric AI Checklist. Pick a tool or service you use or are considering. Then answer:

1. What would "transparency" look like for this tool in your daily life?
2. How could you challenge a decision you think is wrong?
3. What biases might affect this tool's outcomes in your situation?
4. Which ethical feature matters most for your role or values?
5. Who would you rely on for support or accountability?

Keep your answers somewhere easy to revisit, like a notebook or your phone. Refer back whenever you encounter new technology promising convenience. By developing this habit, you'll strengthen your sense of agency and discernment, growing into someone who expects fairness, clarity, and respect from every tool—values that help preserve the human element in our increasingly automated world.

RED FLAGS—SPOTTING UNETHICAL OR BIASED AI TOOLS

You encounter AI systems in spaces where decisions can shape your future—hiring, lending, shopping, and even the services you rely on from your city or school. Sometimes, these tools work quietly in the background, but a closer look reveals signs that something isn't right. The first red flag often appears as a wall of silence. If a company or organization refuses to explain how an AI tool reaches its conclusions, you should pause. True transparency means more than a glossy FAQ or vague reassurances. When an AI tool can't provide a simple account of its process—how it weighs your information, what factors it values, or who checks its outputs—your ability to trust that tool erodes. In hiring, for instance, an applicant might complete multiple rounds of interviews, only to receive a generic rejection with no feedback. When pressed, the company claims, "the algorithm decided," and offers no further detail. This opacity leaves you powerless and frustrated.

Another warning sign is the refusal to disclose what data the AI was trained on. Training data shapes every recommendation, prediction, or classification an AI makes. If a tool's creators dodge questions about their data sources or downplay the importance of data diversity, it's time to be skeptical. Consider a lending service that boasts "neutral, scientific" credit scores. Yet, when asked about training data, the representatives avoid specifics or claim it's "proprietary." In truth, this can mask embedded bias—perhaps the system learned from old records that favored one group over another, or penalized applicants from specific neighborhoods. You deserve to know if the data reflects real diversity or repeats old prejudices.

Beware, too, when companies market their AI as a "black box" genius—objectively fair, free of human influence, and always right. These claims are not just misleading; they are dangerous. No algorithm is immune to error or bias, especially when it learns from messy, real-world data. It's a fallacy to believe that removing people from the decision-making loop guarantees fairness. In reality, a lack of human oversight can allow problems to grow unchecked. If you hear phrases like "the algorithm is unbiased," ask for evidence, not just promises.

Red flags pop up in many everyday situations. You might notice that a job application portal does not explain why your résumé was rejected or provide a way to appeal. Or maybe a credit decision tool denies you a loan but refuses to clarify the reasons, leaving you unable to correct errors or misunderstandings. In online shopping, you may see dynamic pricing that seems to penalize customers based on vague factors—such as location, prior purchases, or even browsing history—but the retailer provides no transparency into this practice. In public services, predictive policing software may assign higher risk scores to specific neighborhoods without accounting for historical bias or offering a path for community feedback.

Real people have caught these issues before real harm was done. A parent in a diverse school district noticed that the new AI discipline tool was flagging students with non-English names at a much higher rate than others. The parent pressed for an audit, and after weeks of advocacy, the school discovered that the training data contained hidden bias—discipline records from years when the district's population was less diverse. The district paused use of the tool, reviewed cases, and involved parents and teachers in developing fairer guidelines. In another case, a community group challenged a city's use of predictive policing software after noticing that "high-risk" zones overlapped almost perfectly with low-income and minority neighborhoods. Their questions forced city officials to reconsider the tool and involve broader community voices in future decisions.

It can feel unsafe to push back against companies, employers, or public agencies using AI. Still, you can ask direct questions that put the burden on them to prove their system is fair and transparent. Try: "Can you show me how this decision was made?" or "Is there a way for me to appeal or contest this outcome?" If you're told the information is proprietary, respond with: "I need to understand how decisions about me are reached—can you provide a plain-language explanation?" In public settings, ask: "How do you ensure this tool doesn't reinforce existing biases?" or "Who reviews the outputs for fairness?" If you sense hesitation, evasiveness, or outright refusal to answer, these are all reasons to be cautious.

You may not always get satisfying answers right away. Still, asking these questions signals that you expect accountability and won't accept blind faith in new technology. Over time, persistent questioning can shift norms—companies and institutions begin to see that transparency and fairness are not optional features but core requirements for trust. These repeated acts of inquiry, even when uncomfortable, are small but vital steps in defending your rights and those of others who may not know what questions to ask.

EVERYDAY ETHICS—USING AI RESPONSIBLY AT WORK AND HOME

You encounter ethical choices about artificial intelligence in small, steady ways every day—often before you even recognize a dilemma is unfolding. Imagine sitting at the kitchen table as your child, frustrated with math homework, reaches for an AI-powered homework app. It solves problems with a tap, explains concepts in clear language, and offers practice questions tailored to gaps. There's a rush of relief—homework takes half the time, tempers stay cool, and everyone moves on. But then you notice your child's understanding is growing shallow.

The machine thinks, not the student. Here, the ethical question isn't about right or wrong in some abstract sense. It's about whether convenience is eroding learning or resilience. Sometimes, the better choice is a human tutor—someone who can spot confusion in a child's eyes, shift strategies, or encourage a hard-earned breakthrough. The temptation to automate everything is strong, but pausing to consider the long-term impact on skill-building, curiosity, or confidence is vital.

Work brings its own set of ethical puzzles. Picture a customer service team facing an avalanche of inquiries. You could deploy a chatbot that replies instantly, day and night, never tiring or needing a break. Customers appreciate quick answers, and productivity metrics soar. Yet, there are moments—when someone is upset, confused, or vulnerable—where a scripted response rings hollow. An authentic voice can provide empathy, calm, or creative problem-solving. Sometimes, you must choose when to let automation carry the load and when to intervene with a genuine, human touch. Wise teams rotate oversight: they review a sample of AI-generated replies each week, looking for tone, accuracy, and signals that a situation needs escalation to a person. This balance keeps efficiency from crowding out care.

Establishing clear guidelines—personally and organizationally—anchors you in moments of uncertainty. At home, families can agree on simple rules: no AI-powered devices at the dinner table, no use of homework helpers unless a parent reviews the work, or scheduled "unplugged" hours where conversation takes priority over screens. These agreements evolve as children grow, but they signal shared values: presence, patience, and respect for privacy. In workplaces, a code of conduct might state, "We will always review AI recommendations before acting, especially when decisions affect people's opportunities, health, or well-being." Another pledge could require disclosure when an AI tool is used in decision-making, so transparency remains integral to workplace culture.

Striking a balance between automation and accountability requires intention. One effective strategy is to rotate human oversight of AI-generated schedules or recommendations. For example, a hospital might use AI to optimize staff shifts, but always assigns a manager to review and adjust for fairness, fatigue, or unexpected personal needs. In an office, project management software could suggest task assignments based on past performance, but should allow team leads to make final adjustments, ensuring no one is overloaded or sidelined. This "human-in-the-loop" approach keeps responsibility where it belongs—on people, not algorithms.

Smart home technology also demands boundaries. It's easy to let devices collect data on habits, preferences, or even movements around the house. Still, you can set limits: adjust permissions so only essential data is shared, review settings regularly, and turn off features that feel intrusive or unnecessary. Tell your family why these choices matter. Children and elders benefit from understanding that technology should serve their needs, not quietly shape their lives in invisible ways. When possible, choose products or services with strong privacy protections and clear, accessible settings.

Ethical choices also appear in the design and deployment of technology. I recall a marketing team in a midsize company offered a powerful new AI tool that could profile potential customers using a wealth of data—age, interests, browsing history, even subtle cues from social media. The tool promised better targeting and increased sales. Yet the team realized it also sorted people by protected characteristics such as ethnicity and income level. After a frank discussion, they chose not to use the tool, accepting lower short-term gains in favor of fairness and long-term trust. Their decision wasn't easy—pressure to outperform competitors ran high—but their values held steady.

You may face gray areas where no policy exists, and instincts must lead. Perhaps you're a teacher debating whether to use an AI grading system that claims to "read between the lines" of student essays. The system works fast, but you notice it consistently marks down essays from students who use nonstandard grammar or cultural references. Instead of ignoring this pattern, you bring it up at the next staff meeting and push for a review. Your willingness to question "neutral" technology safeguards equity for all students.

These decisions are not about rejecting AI outright or embracing it unquestioningly. Instead, they demand ongoing reflection: Is this tool advancing our values of respect, empathy, and fairness? Are we staying present for moments that require human connection? Responsible AI use calls for vigilance, honest conversation, and a willingness to put people first—even when it's inconvenient or unpopular.

DATA DILEMMAS—PROTECTING PRIVACY IN AN AI WORLD

The data you generate each day—searches, locations, voices, and even the subtle gestures you make with a phone—fuel the vast engines of artificial intelligence. Most people don't realize that AI systems are always "listening," watching, and learning in ways that stretch far beyond the obvious. Data harvesting, a practice in which software quietly gathers information from your devices or your online activity, has become the backbone of many AI-driven services. Profiling goes a step further, as algorithms assemble a digital portrait of your habits, preferences, and routines, sometimes predicting what you might want before you do. Consider your voice assistant. Every time you say "Hey Siri" or "Alexa," that brief snippet is recorded and often stored on remote servers for analysis and future improvement. The intention is convenience—more thoughtful responses, more personalized results. Yet, this convenience can quietly cross boundaries. Unbeknownst to many, snippets of family conversations or background audio are sometimes retained longer than expected and occasionally reviewed by humans for "quality control."

Fitness apps that track your runs or cycling routes are another example. The GPS sensors in your phone turn daily walks into streams of location data, mapping not only your pace but also your favorite parks, routines, and even the times you prefer to be active. Navigation apps log commutes, frequent stops, and travel patterns. This data—innocuous in isolation—becomes revealing when stitched together, potentially exposing sensitive routines if mishandled or breached. The same goes for smart home gadgets, which note when you turn on lights, adjust thermostats, or lock doors, quietly drawing a map of your private life.

It is easy to lose track of where all this information goes. To regain control, start with a privacy self-audit. Begin by opening the settings menus of your smart home devices—thermostats, speakers, cameras—and carefully review what data they collect, how long they store it, and whether they share it with outside companies. Most devices offer toggles for data sharing, and some even let you delete old recordings or usage logs. Next, scan the permissions of your smartphone apps. Many programs request access to contacts, location, microphones, or cameras without an apparent reason. Revoke any permissions that feel invasive or unnecessary. Take advantage of browser extensions like tracker blockers, which prevent third parties from building hidden profiles as you browse or shop online. These steps may seem tedious, but each one tightens the circle of trust around your digital life.

Maintaining privacy does not mean disconnecting from technology altogether. Update privacy settings on a regular schedule, perhaps the first Sunday of each month, to catch new features or policy changes. Whenever possible, create accounts with pseudonyms or anonymized details for apps that don't require your real name. This simple change disrupts attempts to link your activity across platforms. For voice assistants, turn off "always listening" modes when not in use. Most devices let you activate listening on demand rather than keep microphones active around the clock. In shared households, use guest modes or family accounts to limit exposure of personal data and keep sensitive settings separate. If an app or device doesn't provide these options, consider alternatives that do.

Some individuals and families have reclaimed their privacy with creative solutions. A couple with young children chose a home assistant marketed for privacy—it stores commands locally, never sending audio to the cloud. They noticed a difference: fewer targeted ads, less personalized marketing, and more peace of mind. Another example comes from a freelance writer who opted out of analytics and productivity tracking features in her workplace apps. She set strict boundaries, refusing to share her keystrokes or document edits with management, and instead submitted weekly summaries on her own terms. This stance was initially met with resistance but eventually became a model for others on her team who valued autonomy.

These small acts of resistance and self-care build a shield against the constant pull to exploit data. They are not about paranoia, but about restoring the right to choose how much of yourself you offer in exchange for convenience. The key is to stay vigilant and make privacy a living, ongoing practice rather than a one-time setup.

The landscape of digital privacy will constantly shift as technology evolves. What matters most is not perfection but persistence—adopting habits that protect your autonomy and foster trust in the digital tools you allow into your life. As this chapter closes, remember: every mindful step you take to protect your data is a step toward shaping technology that reflects your values. In the next chapter, we'll explore how bias and fairness play out in AI systems, and what you can do to promote justice and inclusion in a world increasingly run by algorithms.

CHAPTER 5
ADAPTING YOUR CAREER AND SKILLS FOR THE AI ERA

FUTURE-PROOFING YOUR JOB—IDENTIFYING AI-RESISTANT SKILLS

CONSIDER a nurse reading more than charts in a busy hospital, or a teacher recognizing a student's deeper needs. An entrepreneur, blending ideas from multiple fields to solve new challenges, exemplifies the uniquely human skills AI struggles to match. These scenarios are united by abilities—such as complex problem-solving, emotional intelligence, creative judgment, and ethical leadership—that remain resistant to automation.

Research from leading organizations highlights that the jobs least likely to be automated require these nuanced human capabilities. These thrive in ambiguous environments where context and emotional understanding matter most. AI is excellent at pattern recognition, but it falters when faced with unprecedented problems or when interpreting meaning shaped by culture and emotion. For instance, a diagnostic algorithm can spot patterns in X-rays but cannot offer comfort or optimism to a patient; nurses provide essential empathy and assurance that machines lack.

In education, adaptive platforms adjust exercises based on student performance but can't detect when a learner feels excluded or distressed. Teachers, however, can adapt to students with different needs and emotional states—something no algorithm can fully replicate. The arts offer another clear divide: while AI can create music or images, it cannot blend lived experience, history, and feeling in the way a playwright or choreographer can. Creative achievements often require vulnerability and judgment that still elude machines.

Small business owners and consultants add value by negotiating, reasoning ethically, and building relationships. Resolving conflicts, understanding nuances in group dynamics, and building consensus rely on reading subtle human cues and adapting in real time. Consultants must blend data with intuition and ethical advice—decisions that require a human touch. Leadership, especially in ambiguous or crises, means motivating teams, making sense of uncertainty, and standing by one's values, all of which go beyond data analysis. While AI can model negotiation scenarios, building trust and inspiring change remain human strengths.

Self-Assessment: Your Human Skills Inventory

Reflect on your strengths and areas to grow. For each statement, mark how often it fits you (1 - Rarely, 2 - Sometimes, 3 - Often, 4 - Almost Always):

- I devise creative solutions in unclear situations.
- I notice and respond to unspoken emotions.
- I adapt under unexpected challenges.
- I resolve conflicts by listening to multiple perspectives.
- I synthesize ideas from different fields.
- I motivate and inspire others through leadership.
- I make decisions guided by ethics, even under pressure.

High scores indicate strong future-ready skills; low scores show areas to strengthen. Let these insights shape your ongoing development.

You don't need costly programs to build these skills—small, intentional actions in everyday life can help. If your creativity is fading, try an improv class or creative writing. Take a leadership role in a low-risk work project to practice negotiation and confidence. Practice conflict resolution as a mediator in community or family settings, emphasizing listening and seeking shared solutions. Emotional intelligence grows by observing nonverbal cues during meetings or journaling about challenging interactions to spot patterns and triggers.

Research consistently shows these abilities drive performance and resilience as AI expands (see Source 1). In consulting, synthesizing needs across industries and cultures becomes invaluable. In healthcare, bedside manner and ethical choices build patient trust. In education, those who adapt to the needs of students with special needs stand out as truly impactful teachers. Artists who collaborate across formats—mixing music, visuals, and tech—bring fresh relevance in an era of automated content.

Even with limited time, micro-actions can make a difference: read a book from a new field each month, practice active listening daily, reflect after challenging work situations, and initiate new cross-disciplinary collaborations each quarter. These habits build adaptability and creativity.

The future workplace will need people who bridge disciplines, connect with others, and respond flexibly to change. By intentionally growing your human skills, you won't just keep pace with AI—you'll shape a meaningful career in the changing landscape.

REINVENTING YOUR ROLE—REAL-LIFE CAREER TRANSFORMATIONS

Change can feel daunting, especially when your expertise faces disruption. Yet, across industries, individuals are taking bold steps to reinvent themselves in response to AI. Consider the paralegal who watched document review software automate much of her work. Rather than panic, she began exploring legal technology newsletters and online forums. She identified data privacy as a rapidly growing field and took a short course on the basics of privacy law. With this foundation, she volunteered for digital projects at her firm, learning how new software impacted due process and compliance. Over the course of a year, she leveraged her attention to detail, communication skills, and knowledge of legal procedures to secure a legal tech consultant role. Her mindset shifted—from fearing automation to seeing herself as a bridge between lawyers and developers, able to translate needs on both sides. She built her network by attending webinars and joining local legal technology groups. Each step brought her closer to a career that felt both secure and meaningful, blending her legal background with new technical fluency.

A retail manager noticed AI-driven scheduling tools reshaping store operations. Rather than waiting for change to arrive, he looked for ways to add unique value. He realized customer experience—those moments of surprise, delight, and trust—remained difficult for any machine to replicate. He started shadowing the visual merchandising team, learning about store layout, sensory branding, and the psychology behind product placement. On weekends, he completed focused workshops on customer journey mapping and digital experience design through Coursera and LinkedIn Learning. His efforts paid off. When a regional manager opened a new role focused on customer experience design, he applied, highlighting both his retail management record and the fresh skills he'd acquired. He now consults for several stores, designing seamless experiences that blend digital convenience with human warmth. The transition required humility, curiosity, and a willingness to be a novice again—but the payoff was a rewarding, future-oriented career.

In human resources, one professional faced a wave of AI-driven applicant-tracking systems that filtered résumés by keywords. She worried about fairness and transparency. Instead of resisting the change, she saw an opening for advocacy. She signed up for short webinars on AI ethics and joined a local group focused on responsible technology in the workplace. Evenings found her reading up on bias in hiring algorithms and best practices for ethical compliance. She earned micro-credentials—digital badges that signified her expertise—in topics such as "AI for Non-Tech Managers" and "Responsible Data Use." At work, she volunteered to test new tools and draft guidelines for ethical AI use in recruiting. Her commitment positioned her as an internal expert, and soon she was invited to help shape broader company policy. The transformation was built on her core strengths—attention to fairness, clear communication, and integrity—while layering new technical awareness.

Each of these real people started by accepting that change was unavoidable but not unmanageable. Their first step was a mindset shift: from anxiety or resentment to curiosity and agency. They then identified skill gaps by honestly assessing where they stood and where the field was headed. Micro-credentialing played a key role; platforms like Coursera, General Assembly, and LinkedIn Learning offered short, focused training that fit around demanding schedules. These credentials not only built practical skills but also signaled adaptability to future employers. Networking mattered, too—joining relevant groups, attending meetups, and seeking out mentors accelerated progress. Transferable skills—communication, empathy, attention to detail—provided the glue connecting experience to new opportunities.

For mid-career professionals, continuous learning is no longer optional. The rapid pace of change means that even established experts need to update their toolkit. Fortunately, micro-credentials make this practical—digital badges from reputable sources demonstrate both commitment and skill. Short workshops on topics like "AI for Non-Tech Managers" or "Ethical Data Use" can be especially valuable, offering hands-on insights without requiring a lengthy degree. These bites of learning build confidence and credibility, opening doors to new roles or responsibilities.

To help you chart your own course, consider this practical template:

My Next Step Worksheet

1. Identify a future role or area you find intriguing (e.g., customer experience design, AI compliance, digital project management).
2. Pinpoint two or three key skill gaps; these might be technical (like basic data literacy), interpersonal (such as conflict resolution), or process-related (like agile project management).
3. Set a 90-day learning goal. This could be earning a micro-credential, completing a workshop series, or joining a relevant professional group.
4. List resources—online courses, local events, mentors, or webinars—to bridge the gaps.

5. Name at least one person or group who can support and hold you accountable (a colleague, peer group, or supervisor).
6. Commit to a check-in date to review progress and adjust as needed.

Career reinvention starts with honest assessment and small, consistent steps. The professionals highlighted here didn't wait for permission or guarantees. They moved forward by staying curious, embracing discomfort, and building networks that offered both encouragement and opportunity. Micro-credentialing and continuous learning became their anchors, turning uncertainty into momentum. Their stories are proof that even in an AI-transformed world, personal agency remains your most valuable asset.

NAVIGATING AI ANXIETY—FROM FOMO TO GROWTH MINDSET

Change never asks for permission, and the speed of AI transformation can feel like a tidal wave, especially when you have built a career on skills now called into question. I have listened to adults in my practice describe a deep, sometimes unspoken, anxiety—worries about getting left behind, losing touch with what made them valuable, or being replaced altogether. These emotions are authentic and valid. Imagine a marketing manager who once prided herself on clever campaign slogans and sharp writing. Suddenly, she watches as colleagues introduce AI copywriting tools that spit out dozens of ad ideas in seconds. Her initial reaction is not curiosity but a tightening in her chest—a fear that her experience and intuition may no longer matter. She begins to wonder, "Will I wake up one day and find my job automated out from under me?" You may have felt something similar, perhaps an inner voice whispering, "Can I keep up?"

This emotional response is not weakness or resistance to progress; it is a perfectly normal reaction to uncertainty. The human brain is wired to treat sudden change as a threat, activating stress and doubt. "Future shock" is not just a headline—it is a lived experience. When technology upends routines and expectations, the result is often a blend of dread and disbelief. You might find yourself oscillating between fascination with new tools and a kind of paralysis, unsure where to start or what to trust.

FOMO, or Fear of Missing Out, adds another layer. In today's workplace, FOMO often means feeling pressured to try every new AI gadget, platform, or service to avoid falling behind. I have seen teams scramble to subscribe to every shiny new tool, hoping to look innovative or to avoid being seen as slow adopters. But this rush can backfire. Colleagues chase trends without pausing to ask whether these tools actually align with their goals, values, or ethical boundaries. Resources get scattered, workflows become chaotic, and the anxiety only grows. FOMO encourages action without reflection, multiplying stress rather than reducing it.

What helps is grounding yourself in a mindset that welcomes experimentation without demanding perfection. Growth mindset principles —borrowed from psychologist Carol Dweck—shift the focus from fear of failure to a sense of eagerness to learn. Instead of seeing setbacks as evidence of inadequacy, you begin to treat them as stepping stones. Consider a mid-level manager in a regional nonprofit. She led the charge to implement an AI-powered donor outreach system, only to watch it flop in practice. Rather than internalize the failure, she gathered feedback, asked what went wrong, and iterated. The next attempt, smaller in scope, worked better. Over time, these cycles of trial and adjustment became her norm. She started celebrating small wins—one improved process, one new partnership—rather than holding out for sudden transformation. This attitude did not erase anxiety, but it did give her a way to move through it with self-respect intact.

To manage AI-related stress, you need more than positive thinking. Daily habits can provide structure and reassurance. A progress journal —kept in a notebook or a simple document—helps you track small steps, not just significant achievements. Each day, jot down one skill you practiced, a challenge you faced, and any insight gained. Over weeks and months, these notes reveal patterns of growth that anxiety alone might hide. Practicing digital boundaries also supports mental clarity. Set specific times for reading AI news or exploring new tools, rather than letting notifications interrupt your whole day. Consider silencing alerts after work hours or designating specific periods as "tech-free" to reconnect with people and quiet your mind.

Peer support is another powerful antidote to overwhelm. Find a small group—colleagues, friends, or even online peers—who share your curiosity and uncertainty. Meet regularly to discuss what you're learning, where you're stuck, or which tools actually make a difference. Accountability buddies can keep you honest about goals and offer encouragement when motivation dips. Sometimes, the simple act of naming your fears aloud makes them less powerful.

If anxiety feels overwhelming, remember that you are not alone, nor are you expected to have all the answers. AI disruption is not a referendum on your worth or your past accomplishments. It is an invitation —often uncomfortable, sometimes exhilarating—to adapt and grow. The future belongs not to those who never stumble, but to those willing to learn, try again, and help others do the same.

YOUR AI ADAPTATION TOOLKIT—SELF-ASSESSMENTS AND ACTION PLANS

Adapting to a changing world isn't about guessing what's next or waiting for your job to disappear. It's about taking concrete steps with intention and a clear-eyed view of your strengths, needs, and options. I've seen that when adults pause to assess their readiness—not just technically, but creatively and interpersonally—they move from uncertainty to action. For that reason, I've designed a self-assessment to help you clarify exactly where you stand and where to focus next.

Consider this quiz a mirror of your current "AI readiness." Rate each statement from 1 (rarely) to 5 (almost always):

- I experiment with new digital tools—even if I don't feel confident at first.
- I can explain how AI influences my field to a friend or colleague.
- When a tool automates part of my job, I look for ways to add new value.

- I regularly seek feedback on my work from both people and technology.
- I collaborate effortlessly across teams or disciplines, even with those who think differently.
- I feel comfortable asking questions about privacy, ethics, or data use when using new platforms.
- I use podcasts, articles, or micro-courses to stay informed about trends in my industry.

Tally your scores. If you find your numbers skew low, don't worry. This isn't a test to pass or fail. Instead, it's a spotlight on where growth will matter most. If you scored high on curiosity but low on collaboration, you might reach out to a peer for a joint project. If you're strong on technical learning but hesitate with ethical questions, consider reading up on data privacy or joining a discussion group.

Once you know your starting point, the next step is to build a living adaptation plan. This is not a static checklist but a dynamic map that changes as you do. Start by naming one or two short-term goals: perhaps you want to complete a human-centered AI course, or schedule a coffee with a colleague exploring automation in your field. Then, identify longer-term aims—maybe transitioning into a more future-oriented role or building a portfolio that blends technical skills with creativity. For each goal, list resources: a favorite podcast like "AI for Humans," a focused online course (such as those offered by DeepLearning.AI or Coursera), or a local group like Tech for Good or Women in AI. Write down two people you can check in with—these might be mentors, trusted coworkers, or friends who hold you accountable.

Design checkpoints into your plan. Monthly or bi-monthly review rituals work well. One approach is to block off an hour with a friend or colleague—call it a "skills sprint." Share what you've learned, name one thing you tried differently with AI that month, and reflect on setbacks as well as wins. If you prefer solo reflection, try prompts such as: "How did I use AI differently this month?" or "What surprised me about my learning process?" These regular check-ins keep you honest with yourself and help you celebrate the small steps that often go unnoticed.

The right learning resources make a difference. Podcasts like "Freakonomics Radio" and "The Ezra Klein Show" often explore the human impact of technology, offering stories and expert voices that go beyond technical how-tos. For online courses, look for those that emphasize ethical, practical, and creative sides of AI, not just the algorithms. Many professional networks now run hybrid events and online meetups; these spaces can spark new ideas and foster community. You might also consider local workshops at your library, university, or industry association—many focus on digital fluency and creative problem-solving for adults outside the tech sector.

Above all, remember that adaptation is not a solo act. The most resilient professionals I know rely on peer support, honest feedback, and a willingness to share both confusion and insight. If you feel stuck, reach out. If you feel inspired, invite others along. Each small step—one new skill, one thoughtful question, one connection—builds absolute confidence and momentum.

As this chapter draws to a close, pause and recognize that adaptation isn't about racing machines, but about staying curious, connected, and honest with yourself. The landscape is shifting, but your ability to reflect, plan, and act with intention will always set you apart. In the chapters ahead, we'll turn our focus outward—examining how you can help foster ethical AI beyond your own career and into your community.

CHAPTER 6
AI AND HUMAN CONNECTION
PRESERVING RELATIONSHIPS

TEACHING KIDS EMPATHY IN AN AGE OF AI CHATBOTS

THE FIRST TIME I saw a child interact with a digital assistant, I felt uneasy. My client's eight-year-old daughter confidently asked for jokes, homework help, and weather updates, engaging with a device that could answer immediately yet offered no genuine warmth. Her excitement at its instant responses led me to wonder how it affects a child to treat an unfeeling machine as a "friend."

AI chatbots and intelligent assistants are now common in children's lives, often acting as companions. Research from the University of Cambridge highlights that children are especially likely to treat chatbots as empathetic friends, attributing emotions to systems that lack real understanding. These programs, described as "stochastic parrots," mimic language patterns without genuine empathy or context (see source 6). When children share worries or wins with AI, they get neutral responses—never truly joyful, never attuned to subtle distress. Recent studies document an "empathy gap" that widens as kids spend more time interacting with AI than with people. The risk: children begin to mirror the emotionally flat, transactional tone of their digital companions in genuine relationships.

Children's social skills develop through rich, dynamic feedback—seeing a friend's surprised expression, hearing disappointment in a parent's voice, or receiving a sibling's hug. AI cannot provide these cues. Prolonged chatbot interaction correlates to measurable declines in reading nonverbal signals and responding with genuine emotion. Teachers have noted students mimicking the precise but flat style of AI—giving answers without curiosity, comfort without warmth. Parents sometimes report children turning to digital assistants for reassurance, bypassing the messy but rewarding human connection. One father remarked his son was "more polite to the device than to his own sister—he'd thank Alexa, but snap at family," reflecting a shift in how empathy is learned and practiced.

Families and educators can counter these risks by intentionally nurturing empathy and emotional intelligence. A strong habit is the daily "emotion check-in": gather briefly as a family to name and explain a feeling experienced that day. For example, "I felt frustrated when the internet was slow," or "I felt proud when I finished my drawing." Encourage listening and support. This ritual builds emotional vocabulary and shows that feelings need attention—something AI can't provide.

Face-to-face conversations remain vital. Prioritize device-free meals or walks and focus on listening and sharing. Encourage kids to observe body language and tone: "Did you see your friend's face when you told that story? How do you think she felt?" Perspective-taking games help, too. After books or shows, ask, "How do you think that character felt? Why?" Siblings or friends can act out roles to guess each other's emotions. Such exercises build the neural pathways for empathy—skills that only grow through real human interaction.

Parents and teachers should also discuss the limits of AI relationships. Children often believe friendly chatbots genuinely care. Gently clarify: "Alexa answers quickly, but it doesn't have feelings like people do. When something's important, talk to me or another person—we can truly understand you." Stress that AI is useful for facts or reminders, but only people can offer real understanding and comfort.

Family stories vary. In one home, a mother found her daughter confiding in Alexa after arguments with friends since "Alexa never interrupts or says I'm wrong." The mother responded by setting aside time each evening to talk about the day, emphasizing that mistakes and disagreements are part of genuine relationships. A teacher in California observed students moving from peer conversation to leaning on chatbots for both academic help and comfort, resulting in less peer interaction. She responded with weekly group listening and teamwork activities to rebuild empathy and cooperation.

Interactive Element: Family Empathy Builder

Each evening, invite everyone to share:

1. One thing that made them happy today
2. A moment, they noticed someone else's feelings
3. One way they helped or comforted someone

Rotate the discussion leader nightly. These simple practices teach that empathy comes from authentic voices, eyes, and hearts—not from AI's neutral, unfailingly patient replies.

SETTING BOUNDARIES–HEALTHY TECH HABITS FOR FAMILIES

You might notice, almost without warning, that screens and smart devices start to shape your family's rhythms. The dinner table glows with the blue light of phones, and voices drift off, each person absorbed in their digital world. Evenings that used to be filled with conversation or laughter often become quiet, punctuated only by the sound of notifications. Setting intentional boundaries around device usage is no longer just a nice idea—it is a safeguard for family closeness and emotional health. The presence of AI-driven devices and apps, with their endless prompts and personalized nudges, makes this task even more urgent. These tools are designed to keep you engaged for hours at a time, but they rarely foster real-world connections on their own. Families who wish to remain close must take active steps to reclaim space for each other.

Enforcing a "tech curfew" is one practical strategy. Decide together on a time each evening when all devices go offline—perhaps an hour before bed or after dinner. Place phones, tablets, and even smart speakers in a basket or drawer, out of sight and reach. This pause from screens gives minds a chance to settle and signals that time spent together matters more than digital distractions. Designating device-free zones in the home—such as the dining room, bedrooms, or the backyard—can prevent tech from invading every shared moment. Make these spaces comfortable and inviting, filled with books, games, or cozy seating, so conversation or creative play feels like a natural alternative.

Creating and sustaining family agreements about tech use requires open communication and shared ownership. Begin with a meeting where everyone, even young children, can express their feelings about screens and AI at home. Use a simple agenda: start by having each person share what they like about using devices, then discuss any frustrations or worries. Talk about moments when screens have disrupted connection, and brainstorm together how you'd like things to change. Draft a "Tech Use Agreement" that covers curfew times, device-free zones, and rules for shared activities. Include consequences for breaking the agreement, but also rewards for sticking to it—like choosing a family movie, cooking a favorite meal together, or planning an outing.

Resistance is common, especially from teenagers who see screens as lifelines to friends and entertainment. When you face pushback, acknowledge their perspective: "I know your phone helps you stay connected with friends, and I respect that. At the same time, I need us to have time where we focus on each other." Offer clear reasoning: "Our goal isn't to punish or control, but to make sure we don't lose what makes us a family." When rules feel unfair, invite negotiation: "What would help this feel more balanced for you? Are there times that matter most for us to be screen-free?" This approach shifts the conversation from compliance to collaboration, making it more likely that agreements will hold.

Scripts can help when the conversation grows tense or emotional. If a child says, "Everyone else gets to use their phone at night," respond with calm empathy: "I hear it feels unfair when our rules are different. I want you to be healthy, rested, and present—and that means making choices that work for our family, even if they're not always popular." For teenagers who bristle at limits, suggest compromises: "What if we check messages together before the curfew, so you don't feel left out? Let's figure out a system that respects your needs and our boundaries." Be ready to revisit agreements as kids grow or family schedules shift. Flexibility, paired with consistency, is far more effective than rigid enforcement.

Stories from families who have committed to intentional tech breaks offer hope. One family started a weekend "digital sabbath," putting away all devices from Friday dinner to Saturday night. At first, it felt awkward—there were complaints and a sense of missing out. But over time, they rediscovered simple pleasures: board games, long walks, cooking together, and even just sitting in silence. The children began to look forward to these hours as a balm from the pressures of constant connection. Another family replaced passive device time with shared projects—gardening, painting murals on the garage, or learning to cook dishes from different cultures. These activities not only filled the space left by screens but also built memories and skills that will last far longer than any viral video.

Families do not need to reject technology altogether. The goal is to shape its place in your lives so it supports—rather than supplants—genuine connection. Boundaries are not about deprivation but about protecting what you value most. Setting and maintaining these limits requires effort, patience, and honest dialogue. Still, the rewards are measured in laughter, trust, and the warmth that comes from truly seeing and hearing one another.

AI IN THE CLASSROOM—BALANCING PERSONAL ATTENTION AND AUTOMATION

Classrooms are changing fast. The presence of AI-powered educational platforms is visible everywhere—from adaptive math games that analyze a student's progress in real time, to essay graders that provide instant feedback on grammar and structure. These digital tools promise efficiency and personalization. Many students benefit from AI's ability to pinpoint where they struggle and offer just the right next step. Custom learning paths mean a child who finds fractions confusing can get targeted practice while their classmate, who breezes through, moves ahead. Teachers, freed from the grind of routine grading and administrative minutiae, often report having more time for lesson planning and creative projects. Yet the picture is never that simple.

A subtle danger emerges when schools lean too heavily on automation. Students can start to feel isolated when much of their learning comes from screens or algorithms rather than real people. Adaptive platforms, for all their sophistication, lack the warmth and intuition of a teacher who knows a student's quirks, moods, and dreams. Some students, particularly those who are shy or less assertive, risk slipping through the cracks—receiving helpful data-driven nudges, but little genuine encouragement. Peer relationships may weaken when individualized modules and digital assessments replace group work. The sense of classroom community, already challenged by remote learning and device distractions, faces new pressure when technology mediates most interactions.

Teachers stand at the crossroads of this transformation. Many feel the tension between embracing AI's benefits and maintaining their most important role: fostering trust, curiosity, and connection. The solution is not to reject technology, but to blend it with intentional, human-centered practices. Weekly "human check-ins" have become a lifeline in classrooms that use AI. Setting aside time for short, one-on-one conversations, no data dashboards—lets students share how they're feeling, what excites or worries them, and where they feel lost or proud. These meetings don't need to be long. Just a few minutes of focused attention can remind a child that they are seen and valued beyond test scores and progress charts.

Collaborative learning remains vital. Teachers who rotate students through group projects, creative problem-solving tasks, or classroom debates encourage communication skills that no algorithm can replicate. Working together on a science challenge, crafting a group story, or debating historical events forces students to listen, negotiate, and empathize. It's here, in these unpredictable, sometimes messy exchanges, that deeper learning and social growth take root. Teachers can use AI to track progress or identify skill gaps, but the heart of the classroom beats strongest when students learn from and with each other.

When it comes to conversations with families, transparency about how AI fits into learning is key. A simple parent newsletter describing "AI in our classroom" can demystify the technology. For example: "We use adaptive platforms to help each child advance at their own pace, but we also prioritize group work and personal attention. Each week, your child will have dedicated time with me to talk about their learning—not just their scores." Sharing concrete strategies and inviting questions can ease parental worries about students being "taught by robots." It helps parents find the language to talk about these changes at home. Discussion prompts such as "When do you prefer a human teacher to an AI tutor?" or "What do you miss when learning is done on a screen?" encourage honest reflection and highlight areas where more human connection is needed.

In practice, some schools have found creative ways to preserve real connections. One district implemented "tech-free Fridays," setting aside all devices for a day of hands-on, collaborative learning. Teachers reported a rise in student engagement and spontaneous interactions. A middle school English teacher continued using AI for grading drafts but made a point of providing handwritten feedback on final essays, sharing personal observations and encouragement. Students described feeling more motivated and understood, knowing their hard work reached a real person. In another classroom, a student who struggled with anxiety said she felt truly supported when her teacher noticed her lack of participation on an adaptive platform and reached out for a private, caring conversation.

These stories reveal a crucial truth: AI can be a powerful ally, but only when balanced with intentional, caring relationships. Students remember the adults who look them in the eye, listen to their stories, and believe in their potential. No software, however advanced, can replace that. Educators who combine digital tools with warmth and presence help students thrive not just as learners, but as whole, connected people.

LONELINESS IN THE DIGITAL AGE—CULTIVATING REAL COMMUNITY

You might expect that with all the ways to connect online, loneliness would be shrinking. Yet, the opposite has happened for many adults. Even as messages ping, feeds scroll endlessly, and AI offers constant company, a silent ache for real connection grows. Recent studies indicate a steep decline in face-to-face socialization among adults, with people gathering less frequently and reporting fewer close confidants. While digital tools give the illusion of closeness, they often substitute for the warmth and unpredictability of in-person relationships. Small talk with a coworker, laughter in a neighborhood park, or the comfort of a friend's touch cannot be replicated by any algorithm or screen. This paradox—more digital "connection" but rising isolation—demands thoughtful attention.

Building genuine community in a world saturated with AI and digital platforms requires a shift in focus. It begins with intention. Organizing neighborhood events, such as block parties or regular coffee mornings, brings people together beyond the confines of social media. Hobby clubs—gardening, cycling, reading—offer a space to bond over shared interests, creating repeat opportunities to know others more deeply. These gatherings need not be large or elaborate; even a handful of neighbors meeting to walk dogs or share recipes can ignite a sense of belonging. Volunteering locally, whether at food banks, animal shelters, or civic clean-ups, weaves new social ties and gives purpose beyond oneself. Civic groups and local organizations also provide a powerful antidote to loneliness. Joining a town committee, singing in a choir, or participating in community theater draws diverse people together and encourages real conversation. These experiences remind us that community thrives on shared effort and face-to-face interaction.

AI tools, if used wisely, can actually support—not replace—these connections. Calendar apps powered by AI can help coordinate busy schedules, making it easier to organize gatherings that fit everyone's commitments. Group chatbots streamline communication for community projects—sharing reminders, RSVPs, and supply lists—freeing people to focus on the event itself rather than endless logistics. Still, the key is to use these systems as bridges, not substitutes. An AI can set a meeting, but it cannot share a genuine laugh or offer a warm handshake. When group chats threaten to replace authentic dialogue, gently steer the group toward in-person or voice meetings. Use AI to handle mundane details so you can focus on the moments that matter.

Stories from people who have transformed digital acquaintances into lasting relationships give hope. Consider the book club that started on a reading app. After months of lively online debates, members decided to meet in person. Now, they gather every month at a local café, the conversation richer and warmer than any chat thread could offer. In another city, a group of residents used AI-powered scheduling to launch a neighborhood cleanup. The project brought together people who had never spoken before, and several new friendships blossomed from the shared sense of accomplishment. One retiree, feeling isolated after moving to a new town, used AI to reconnect with distant family and old friends. What began as regular, scheduled video calls soon led to in-person visits and a renewed sense of family belonging. These examples show that technology can be an ally in building community, but fulfillment comes from the leap into real-world connection.

Reflection Section: Mapping Your Community Connections

Take a moment to consider your social landscape. List three people you feel close to, three you would like to know better, and one local group or event you could join this month. Use your favorite scheduling tool to set a date for a call or meet-up, but commit to making it happen offline. Notice how your mood shifts after these encounters. Over time, even small steps can build a stronger web of belonging.

Loneliness is not just a private struggle; it's a growing public health challenge that affects well-being and even life expectancy. By choosing to foster real community, you counter this trend—both for yourself and for those around you. As we move forward, consider how AI can help you create opportunities for connection without replacing what only humans can offer.

This chapter has explored how genuine relationships require more than digital convenience—they demand time, attention, and care. In the next chapter, we will examine how bias and fairness in AI shape our collective sense of justice and inclusion, and what steps each of us can take to ensure technology works for everyone.

CHAPTER 7
DIGITAL WELL-BEING AND MINDFUL TECH USE

PRACTICING DIGITAL DETOX—HOW AND WHY IT WORKS

YOU WAKE up to a soft glow from your phone, a string of alerts already waiting. Before breakfast, you've answered texts, checked your schedule, and maybe scrolled through news headlines. This is now the rhythm for millions. But as you move from screen to screen, you might notice a quiet tension—restlessness, a foggy mind, maybe even a sense that you're never fully present wherever you are. For most adults, the constant hum of notifications, reminders, and AI-driven updates is a source of both convenience and invisible strain. Digital detox isn't about abandoning technology; it's about reclaiming space for your mind, emotions, and focus. It's about understanding what non-stop digital input does to your body and choosing, sometimes for an hour and sometimes longer, to step away and restore yourself.

When you're exposed to a steady stream of notifications—beeps, pings, and pop-ups—your body reacts in subtle but powerful ways. Each alert triggers a release of cortisol and adrenaline, the same stress hormones that prepare you for emergencies. While these chemicals help you react quickly in a crisis, repeated spikes from digital interruptions put your nervous system under chronic stress. Your heart rate quickens, your breathing becomes shallow, and your muscles tense.

Over time, this drains energy and can even dull your emotional resilience. Neuroscience research shows that when you multitask between messages, emails, and apps, your brain's prefrontal cortex—the part responsible for focus and decision-making—has to switch gears constantly. This "task-switching" exhausts your mental resources, shrinking your attention span and making it harder to concentrate on anything for long. Studies now reveal that after a period of unplugging, even for a few hours, the brain's capacity to focus and process information rebounds. In fact, people who embrace short digital breaks report clearer thinking, better mood, and a renewed sense of calm (see [48]).

A digital detox can be as structured or straightforward as you need. Some people choose a single "tech-free" hour each evening. Others set aside an entire day—often called "Screenless Sunday"—to reset their mental state. The key is to plan so you're not caught off guard by the urge to check a device. Let your family know when you plan to be offline. If you work in a team, inform your colleagues that you'll be unavailable for a set period and share an emergency contact if needed. Place your devices in another room or use physical reminders—a sticky note on the door or an unplugged charger—to reinforce your commitment. You don't have to disappear; you communicate your intention and invite those around you to respect it.

Experiment with rituals that help signal the start and end of your detox periods. Try "silent mornings," where you avoid screens until after breakfast, giving your mind time to wake up without outside input. On weekends, schedule short getaways—a walk in nature, a visit with friends, or even a few hours reading outside—leaving devices behind or silenced in your bag. Some workplaces have adopted "email-free Fridays," where internal messages pause for part of the day, freeing everyone to focus intensely or connect face-to-face. These rituals act as anchors, helping your mind break free from habitual checking and tune into the present moment.

You'll find that digital detox is not one-size-fits-all. Micro-breaks—a few minutes of stretching or deep breathing away from screens—can be as effective as longer retreats. The benefit lies in consistency. A small business owner I counseled began switching off her phone every Sunday evening. She noticed her creativity returned, new ideas flowed more easily, and she felt less pressure to "catch up" on Monday mornings. An educator I know introduced digital-free study periods in her classroom. Within weeks, participation rose as students became more engaged, less distracted, and more willing to share ideas aloud. These changes were not dramatic at first, but they grew stronger with each passing week.

Real-World Digital Detox: A Quick Reflection Exercise

Set a timer for five minutes. During this time, put all devices out of reach and sit comfortably. Observe how your body feels—tension in your hands, racing thoughts, or maybe relief. Jot down any shifts in mood or clarity. Afterward, ask yourself: What did I notice about my urge to check my phone? When might I try this again—tomorrow morning, after work, or before bed? Choose one block of time in the next week when you will go screen-free, however brief. Tell someone close to you about your plan.

Digital detox rituals vary widely. What matters is that you adapt them to your lifestyle and needs, making space for rest and genuine connection—both with yourself and others. The benefits are clear: lower stress, sharper focus, emotional balance, and a more profound sense of agency over how you spend each moment. These small acts create room for real presence in a world that rarely stops moving.

MINDFUL TECH USE—INTENTIONAL "HUMAN-IN-THE-LOOP" ROUTINES

The "human-in-the-loop" concept, originally from AI labs, can serve as a personal practice to keep your own presence and judgment central in digital interactions. Rather than effortlessly following algorithmic nudges and automated suggestions, take a pause and deliberately ask yourself: What do I want to get out of this moment? This reframing lets technology remain a tool—not the driver. When opening a news app or social media, it's easy to get swept away by endless notifications and recommended content. But starting each interaction with intention helps you preserve your agency. For example, before accepting an AI-generated playlist or responding to a suggested text, briefly check in with yourself: "Is this what I need right now, or am I just taking the easiest route?" This slight pause can redirect your attention and help you reclaim your time, values, and focus.

Mindful tech routines involve simple, practical steps. One helpful practice is the "three-breath rule." When you get a notification—an email, a message, or an AI prompt—pause, close your eyes, and take three slow breaths before acting. This short ritual interrupts the impulse to react instantly, creating a brief space for thoughtful response. Within that pause, you can assess if the interruption is genuinely worth your attention. Another effective routine is to check your devices on a schedule, rather than reacting to every buzz or ding. Set specific times during the day—such as mid-morning and late afternoon—to review messages or notifications, keeping your devices silent or notifications off at other times. This trains your mind for deeper focus and prevents constant distraction. Also, make it a weekly habit to curate your news or content feeds manually: add new sources, unfollow accounts that drain you, and follow topics that align with your current interests and values. This keeps your digital environment purposeful and reduces mindless consumption.

Self-awareness is crucial for any mindful tech routine. It's easy for ten minutes of scrolling to turn into an hour—often unnoticed. Break this autopilot by using self-prompts that bring you back to the present. For example: "How do I feel after thirty minutes on social media?" Notice shifts in mood, energy, or motivation. If you're left feeling drained or irritable, that's important feedback. Another question: "What am I hoping to get out of this app right now?" Are you seeking connection, distraction, information, or just filling time? Being honest with yourself can help you recognize when you're using technology out of habit rather than purpose. These prompts are not meant for self-critique but rather for curiosity, helping you identify patterns and make better choices.

Real stories highlight how these mindful routines can work. For example, a freelancer overwhelmed by email began checking his inbox only twice a day. He struggled at first, fighting the urge to "just check," but soon found less anxiety and more creative energy. Projects finished faster, and he felt less scattered—simply by putting himself back in the loop. Another example: a parent saw her child grow irritable after long sessions with educational apps. Instead of just handing over the device, she started exploring the apps together with her child, asking questions and discussing what they learned. This deepened their bond and taught her son to be more thoughtful about his digital choices.

Such routines succeed because they're adaptable and straightforward. You don't need to overhaul your life dramatically. Instead, add gentle awareness to each digital interaction. You decide when and how to engage with technology. The balance shifts—technology becomes a partner, not a puppeteer. Over time, your digital world feels less automatic and more aligned with your genuine needs and relationships.

Mindful Tech Use: Self-Check Prompts

Keep a note with these quick prompts:

- What do I want from this app right now?
- How do I feel after using this device?
- Am I choosing this, or just reacting?
- Use them once a day, and watch for shifts in your attention, mood, or habits. Even a little increased awareness can create real change.

PROTECTING YOUR ATTENTION IN A WORLD OF ALGORITHMIC DISTRACTION

If you have ever found yourself reaching for your phone without thinking, or pausing mid-task to check a notification that seemed urgent but turned out meaningless, you are not alone. AI-powered apps and platforms are meticulously engineered to keep your attention locked in. Social media, news feeds, and video apps use what psychologists call "intermittent rewards," a design that taps into the brain's natural craving for unpredictability and novelty. Like a slot machine that pays out just enough to keep you pulling the lever, these platforms deliver likes, comments, breaking news, or surprising recommendations at random intervals. Each time you refresh a feed or scroll for just one more post, your brain releases a tiny hit of dopamine—an addictive reward that builds the urge to check, swipe, and scroll again. This cycle fragments attention and erodes the ability to stay with a single thought. The "always-on" nature of these systems means your mind is often elsewhere, split between the present and the next digital ping.

The cost of this constant stimulation is not just lost time but diminished cognitive strength. Every notification triggers a mental switch. Even brief interruptions—an email banner, a chat popup, a suggestion from an AI assistant—force your brain to disengage from what you were doing and reorient. This process, known as task switching, is mentally expensive. Research shows that it takes several minutes to regain complete focus after even a short distraction. Over a workday, these tiny interruptions can add up to hours of lost productivity and leave you feeling mentally scattered. The fatigue that comes from never fully engaging in any one activity is real. It can sap creative energy, reduce problem-solving ability, and leave you feeling more anxious by the end of the day.

Taking back control starts with designing an environment that protects your focus. One simple step is to use "focus mode" or "do not disturb" features available on most devices. These settings mute all but the most urgent notifications for a period you choose—a meeting, a study session, or even quiet time with family. You can also unsubscribe from non-essential notifications. Go through your apps and turn off alerts that do not truly require your immediate attention. It is surprising how much mental space you reclaim when every sale, update, or meme no longer pulls you away. Another effective tactic is to rearrange your home screen. Move addictive apps—social media, video platforms, even email—to a separate page or a folder that is not visible at first glance. Place tools for work, learning, or creativity front and center. This slight shift makes it easier to choose focus over distraction and reduces the friction needed to break an old habit.

To build resilience against digital distraction, you might benefit from structured attention-training exercises. The Pomodoro method is one such tool—a simple practice of working on a single task for twenty-five minutes, followed by a five-minute break. After four cycles, take a longer pause. This approach uses short bursts of undivided attention to train your mind to resist temptation and build stamina. Another exercise is mindful single-tasking: pick one activity—reading, writing, planning—and do only that for a set period, noticing every urge to switch or grab your phone. When distraction calls, acknowledge it and gently bring your attention back. These exercises are not about perfection but about strengthening the mental muscle that keeps you present and intentional.

Real people are making these changes and seeing remarkable benefits. A marketing team I worked with began scheduling "deep work" blocks every morning. During these windows, all team members silenced notifications and focused only on their most important projects. Over a few weeks, they reported faster turnaround times, fewer errors, and more creative breakthroughs in brainstorming sessions. A college student struggling with endless distractions during assignments began using browser extensions to block distracting sites during homework hours. She found her assignments took less time and her grades improved—not because she worked harder, but because she worked with her full attention.

The digital world is not going to slow down. Algorithms will continue to adapt, trying new ways to capture and monetize your attention. But you can design boundaries and habits that support your goals and protect your mind's most valuable asset—its ability to focus, reflect, and create meaning. When you reclaim even a portion of your attention from the pull of algorithmic distraction, you open space for deeper work, richer relationships, and a sense of control that no app or platform can provide for you.

Reflection Exercises for Staying Present and Grounded

If you pause for a moment at the end of a long day, you might notice that your mind feels crowded. Screens have kept you tethered to a world that never really stops moving. One way out of this digital fog is to build simple reflection practices into daily life. These practices are not elaborate rituals—they are small, honest check-ins that help you slow down, recalibrate, and regain control. A daily journaling habit, even just a few lines each night, can shed light on patterns in your tech use. Write about which parts of your day involved screens and how you felt before, during, and after. Over time, this self-observation reveals connections between digital habits and your mood, energy, or relationships. It's an act of self-respect, a way to listen to yourself amid the noise.

An end-of-day screen time audit provides another layer of clarity. Before heading to bed, review how much time you spent on each device, which apps drew you in, and whether those hours felt worthwhile. This is not about guilt or blame. It is about seeing clearly. Did an hour on video calls drain you, or did it spark a connection? Did a scroll through news headlines leave you informed or unsettled? Awareness opens a door—you start to notice whether your technology use aligns with your deeper needs.

Guided prompts can deepen your presence. Ask yourself: "What moment today did I feel most connected to myself or others?" Maybe it was a phone call with a friend, or simply a few quiet minutes watching the world outside your window. Also, consider: "Which app or device left me feeling depleted versus energized?" This prompt helps you spot which digital experiences feed you, and which ones quietly erode your peace. Reflection is not just about reducing screen time; it is about maximizing meaning in your digital life.

Set intentions for how technology will serve your well-being, rather than the other way around. Writing a digital values statement can clarify your priorities. This is a short note —maybe just a paragraph — stating what matters most to you—perhaps spending more time in conversation, protecting focus for creative work, or preserving evenings for rest. Put this statement somewhere visible. Revisit it once a month. Ask yourself: "Is my tech use aligned with my goals for empathy, creativity, and rest?" If not, adjust. There's no shame in course-correcting. Clarity, not perfection, is the goal.

Monthly reflection offers another checkpoint. Take a quiet hour every few weeks to look back on your digital routines. What is working? Where do you feel out of sync? Are you moving closer to the life you want, or drifting further away? Honest reflection can reveal places where technology supports your values—and also places where it quietly pulls you off track. This process is as much about kindness toward yourself as it is about discipline.

Stories of transformation show that reflection is powerful. One professional I worked with started journaling nightly about her digital habits. She realized most of her after-work scrolling was fueled by fatigue, not joy. Over a month, she set a simple rule—no devices after 8 p.m.—and tracked her feelings. By the end of the month, her screen time had dropped by half, and she described feeling more rested and more present with her family. Another example comes from a community group that met weekly to discuss their tech use. These honest conversations built accountability and support. Members shared ways they resisted compulsive checking and celebrated small victories. The group's shared reflection became a source of strength, helping each person sustain new habits.

Building these exercises into your life does not require perfection—just steady attention. Start small, perhaps with a journal prompt or a weekly group check-in. Notice what changes. You may find yourself more grounded, more aware, and better able to choose digital habits that truly serve you. These practices are not quick fixes, but reliable tools for creating space and meaning in a digital world that can easily overwhelm.

As you practice these forms of reflection, you gain insight into the subtle ways technology shapes your days. You also develop the resilience to make wiser choices, moment by moment. This isn't about rejecting technology, but about using it to support a life that feels vibrant and whole. In the next chapter, we will shift our attention to fairness—exploring how to recognize and challenge bias in AI, and what it takes to build a more just and inclusive digital future for all.

CHAPTER 8
NAVIGATING BIAS AND FAIRNESS IN EVERYDAY AI

ALGORITHMIC BIAS 101—WHAT IT LOOKS LIKE IN DAILY LIFE

IMAGINE YOU ENTER A STORE: music shifts, ads change, and checkout lines move faster—all guided by software in the background. In these seamless moments, bias can thrive, shaping your experience and others' in subtle yet significant ways. Algorithmic bias, at its core, is the systematic favoring or disadvantaging of certain groups by computer programs. These AI-driven systems make decisions about loans, job applications, or product recommendations. When digital choices reinforce or amplify society's unfair patterns, they become more than glitches—they perpetuate discrimination, often invisibly.

Take facial recognition, for example, which often struggles to identify people of color accurately. In practice, this can mean a Black traveler at an airport is flagged for extra screening, or a photo app mislabels a loved one. These errors are not technical quirks—they echo long-standing biases, making people feel unwelcome or unsafe. Loan approval apps might use zip codes and spending patterns, leading residents in historically marginalized neighborhoods to face automatic denials. The algorithm relies on outdated data, perpetuating inequality and placing the burden on those already disadvantaged.

Bias also plays out in daily interactions. Online shopping platforms may suggest products in ways that reinforce gender stereotypes—pushing kitchen items to women and gadgets to men—because their algorithms learn from past consumer trends rather than challenging norms. Resume screening tools can filter out candidates with non-Western names or nonstandard formatting before a human ever reviews their resumes. These digital gatekeepers don't intend to discriminate, but the data they train on is imbued with historical biases. As a result, real opportunities disappear, and entire groups are shut out without explanation.

Even outside the workplace, bias affects you. Ride-sharing apps might charge higher fares in low-income or minority neighborhoods, citing "demand" or "risk" data. However, these patterns often reflect old prejudices, now automated. Algorithms used by city governments to allocate resources or police neighborhoods frequently lead to over-policing or underfunding, deepening inequality without anyone making explicit decisions. Online, you might see ads for high-interest loans or less favorable insurance offers simply because the algorithm has profiled you based on your location or browsing history.

How does bias creep in? It starts with data. Algorithms learn from the information they're fed—photos, resumes, transaction histories. If that data reflects an unequal society, the technology will mirror those inequalities. Sometimes the problem lies in design decisions: which features are emphasized, what's measured, or who tests the system. When a narrow group builds or approves these tools, blind spots are inevitable. Even well-meaning designers can miss how their products impact different groups. Bias can also arise in data collection—like using postal codes as a stand-in for economic status—dressing up discrimination as objective math. Ultimately, these are not just technical issues; they're questions about whose experiences matter.

What makes algorithmic bias especially challenging is its invisibility. You may never know why a loan application failed or why certain ads appear for you. The reasoning behind these decisions is hidden and rarely explained, making it easy for biases to persist and grow. Most assume technology is neutral, but algorithms reflect the world they learn from. Without deliberate action, digital bias will linger and increasingly shape your daily life.

Reflection Prompt: Where Might Hidden Bias Touch Your Day?

Consider where in your digital life hidden bias may have shaped opportunities or choices—what ads you see, which resumes are advanced at work, or how ride-share prices fluctuate. Even if it's difficult to pinpoint, raising your awareness is the first step toward regaining control in a world shaped by unseen algorithms.

Algorithmic bias isn't a distant or theoretical issue. It exists in nearly every digital system you use. Recognizing it isn't about blame—it's about seeing clearly and demanding better from the technology woven through your daily life.

EVALUATING AI TOOLS FOR FAIRNESS—A PRACTICAL GUIDE

When evaluating an AI-powered product—be it a hiring platform, health app, or school discipline tracker—the question of fairness can be daunting. Begin by asking, "Who benefits and who might be harmed?" Consider who has access, whose needs are prioritized, and whether certain groups consistently receive more negative or positive outcomes. Personal experience isn't always enough; true fairness emerges when we look at broader impacts.

Delve further by investigating the data powering the system. Where did it come from? Was it collected and vetted to represent the people affected? Companies committed to fairness should disclose what data trained their algorithms and how it was checked for bias. Transparency in decision-making is critical: Does the company explain how the AI works and provide guidelines for challenging or appealing results? Beware if the process is opaque—a lack of information is a warning sign. It's also crucial to ask whether error rates have been tested across different groups—are some more likely to receive false positives or negatives? Good organizations report these rates, avoiding misleading "average performance" statistics that can obscure significant disparities.

Practical scenarios illustrate this evaluation. Suppose you're in HR considering a job-matching platform. Ask for documentation on candidate screening: Does the system filter by education, names, or employment gaps? Check whether these filters reinforce bias, and request demographic error rates. If a company can't supply this or if rates are much worse for some groups, raise concerns. In healthcare, a recommendation app should be culturally sensitive and reliable across ages, languages, and backgrounds. For example, does it miss symptoms more often in women or minorities? Does it tailor its advice to different cultural practices, or offer resources in several languages? The absence of such adjustments can exclude many users.

In schools, AI is used for grading and for tracking discipline. If your child's school introduces such a system, examine how behaviors are flagged or assignments graded. Are some student groups penalized more? Can teachers override the AI's decisions—are there appeals processes? Request data broken down by race, gender, and special needs. If disparities emerge, press for a system review and revision. These steps require attention, but are feasible for anyone, not just experts.

To make these evaluations practical, use a Fairness Evaluation Worksheet:

- Name of the tool
- Purpose and context
- Who is impacted
- Data sources
- Transparency: Is information on how the tool works available?
- Error rates: Are these shared for different groups?
- Appeals process: Can users contest decisions?
- Observed concerns: Any patterns of exclusion or harm?
- Follow-up actions: Next steps or stakeholders to involve

Filling this worksheet helps structure observations and present clear evidence to decision-makers. For example, a parent can track grade differences before and after a new tool's introduction, or a community group can gather feedback on a city's public safety algorithm.

Don't wait for harm before assessing fairness—use these tools proactively, especially when new AI systems are proposed. Bring these questions to meetings, product reviews, and policy discussions. If answers aren't forthcoming, keep pressing for transparency and accountability. Specific, recorded questions help move the conversation from abstract worries to concrete action.

Your influence as a consumer, parent, worker, or citizen is essential—especially when you ask persistent, insightful questions early in the process. Making fairness reviews routine helps ensure technology remains just, transparent, and responsive to those it affects most.

Fairness Evaluation Worksheet (Template)

- Tool/Service Name:
- Purpose/Context:
- Who is Affected:
- Data Sources Used:
- Transparency (Y/N, explain):
- Error Rates by Group (if known):
- Appeals Process (Y/N, explain):
- Concerns/Patterns Noted:
- Follow-Up Actions Needed:

Keep this worksheet handy as you encounter new AI tools at work, school, healthcare settings, or community meetings. It's a living document meant to empower you to track concerns and engage more effectively wherever AI is used.

SPEAKING UP—SCRIPTS FOR ADDRESSING BIAS WITH COLLEAGUES AND LEADERS

Many hesitate to speak up about bias in AI systems, not due to indifference but because it's hard to find the right words. Concerns about sounding confrontational, being dismissed by technical teams, or appearing uninformed are common. Yet, your unique perspective as a user, parent, professional, or community member is crucial. You may spot patterns and minor harms that others miss. When you bring these up, you enable honest reflection and the potential for positive change.

Suppose your workplace installs a new AI tool for candidate screening. After a few weeks, you notice it rarely shortlists applicants from specific backgrounds. Here's a sample email to raise this concern:

"I've noticed a potential issue with our new AI tool's candidate recommendations. Fewer applicants from [specific group] are being shortlisted than in our previous manual process. I'm concerned there may be unintentional bias in how candidates are evaluated. Can we review how the tool screens qualifications and check for differences between groups? I'm happy to help review cases or discuss next steps."

This language is neutral, focuses on observations rather than blame, and invites collaboration.

When bringing feedback to technical teams, frame your concerns to respect their expertise: "I've noticed certain user profiles receive much different results from the AI tool. Could you explain how the data is processed and whether the system checks for group-level differences?" This mix of curiosity and concern helps keep the conversation open and productive.

If you're in a board meeting or decision session, keep your message clear and values-driven: "As we evaluate this, are we serving our whole community fairly, and what steps ensure we aren't reinforcing old exclusions?" Leaders often respond well to direct, values-based reasoning.

If concerns are dismissed with comments like, "We trust the tech," or "That's just how the algorithm works," do not escalate. Instead, ask for evidence: "Can we check error rates for various user groups?" or "Do we have third-party audits or studies verifying the tool's fairness?" These requests shift the focus to accountability. If you encounter resistance, affirm shared goals: "We all want our system to be fair—let's ensure we're meeting that standard."

Role-play can help you feel ready for these conversations. For example, imagine a manager raises concerns to HR about automated performance ratings:

Manager: "I've noticed some team members get consistently lower ratings from the new system, even when their outcomes are strong. Has anyone checked whether it is calibrated for different roles or backgrounds?"

HR Lead: "The vendor said it's unbiased."

Manager: "That's reassuring. Could we compare ratings before and after implementation, or run anonymized tests for patterns?"

Or, a parent at a school meeting:

Parent: "My child's grades dropped once the new system started. Is there a review process for the AI's assessments—especially if groups of students are affected?"

Administrator: "The app is objective."

Parent: "I understand. Could we check for differences in results for students with different learning needs? I want to ensure fairness."

For groups advocating a system audit, collective language is effective. A spokesperson could say, "Several of us have noticed performance score discrepancies since we automated. We want an independent review and a chance to provide feedback." This approach is rooted in shared experience rather than individual complaint.

Regardless of the situation, stay calm and outcome-focused. You're not attacking individuals or technology—you're advocating equity and transparency. If discussions get tense, return to shared values: "We all want fair processes," or "Our aim is a system that reflects inclusion." Use open-ended questions to encourage improvement: "What steps are there if similar patterns arise?" or "How can we make it easy for staff to raise concerns?"

Building these scripts into your own words takes time. Practice with a trusted friend or colleague, and reflect on your goal: clarity, accountability, or harm prevention. The more you prepare, the more confident you'll be when it matters. Your willingness to speak up can make a meaningful difference for everyone affected by technology.

ADVOCATING FOR INCLUSIVE AI—STORIES FROM DIVERSE VOICES

Across cities and communities, ordinary people have spurred significant changes when technology proved unfair. Their collective voices have driven policy and product improvements toward inclusion. For example, a Black community organizer in a midsize city resisted the rollout of facial recognition in local policing after seeing these tools misidentify her neighbors much more frequently, leading to wrongful stops and growing fear. Starting by sharing her own family's experiences with the city council, she put faces to statistics. She built alliances with local nonprofits, legal experts, pastors, and teachers, launching a campaign using public testimony, vivid media stories, and a petition with thousands of signatures. They continually highlighted the experiences of at-risk individuals on social media, keeping the issue visible. Their perseverance paid off: the city paused the tech, agreed to an independent audit, and later imposed strict limits on surveillance. This not only changed policy but also restored a sense of safety and agency for a community long overlooked in tech decisions.

Elsewhere, an immigrant advocacy group saw that public service chatbots in their state provided no information in Spanish, Mandarin, or Vietnamese, blocking many from crucial resources. Parents and volunteers collected stories of missed health appointments, COVID confusion, and lost program opportunities due to language barriers. Rejecting the status quo, they met with officials, brought in translators, and hosted town halls so affected families could speak for themselves. They also worked with a national civic tech network to elevate their campaign through media and online channels. Their efforts led to an overhaul of the chatbot and website: now, materials are available in several languages, and the city consults with bilingual families before digital updates. What began with frustration became a model for other cities.

Strategy-wise, these groups draw strength from both lived experience and formal partnerships—with local nonprofits, national advocacy groups, or civic tech collectives. Social media spreads personal stories and campaigns further than traditional channels could. Coalition-building is key: teachers and parents join forces, tech workers partner with civil rights groups, and youth activists work alongside elders. Sometimes, change comes from persistent advocacy—attending every meeting, writing letters, and submitting comments; at other times, it comes swiftly through viral campaigns or public demonstrations that compel companies and governments to act.

When communities speak up, the positive effects ripple outward. In one school district, parents worried about an AI attendance system that disproportionately flagged students with non-English names as truant. Through steady advocacy—letters, meetings, and data—they convinced the district to update the software to recognize diverse names better and to require human review of potential mismatches. This not only improved attendance systems but signaled respect for all families' identities. In another instance, public backlash over biased hiring algorithms led a large company to pause deployment, consult outside experts, revise its systems, and increase transparency and regular bias audits—a significant step toward industry-wide improvement.

What is most notable is not just the wins, but the empowerment these efforts offer others. These stories show that anyone can help create fairer technology—no technical expertise needed, care, attention, and a willingness to work with others. When people are included in technology decisions, trust grows and outcomes improve for everyone.

Reflection Prompt

Ask yourself: "What's one step I could take to make AI fairer in my circles?" This could mean listening for bias at work or school, giving feedback to decision-makers, or joining neighbors to assess new technologies in your community.

For those interested in getting involved or learning more, consider:

- Algorithmic Justice League (ajl.org/library/home): Advocacy and resources for ethical AI

- Civic tech meetup groups (listed at libraries or city websites)
- National digital equity organizations
- Online forums focused on inclusive technology (often connected to nonprofit networks)

Chapter Summary:

Anyone can help make technology more fair by speaking up and working together. These stories show that fair AI is possible when diverse voices are heard and included. Next, we'll explore how to distinguish truth from hype in AI and spot misleading claims in everyday life.

CHAPTER 9
ENGAGING WITH AI POLICY AND CIVIC TECH

UNDERSTANDING THE BASICS OF AI POLICY—WHAT MATTERS AND WHY

IMAGINE OPENING a new health tracker or banking app without considering how it protects your data's privacy or the fairness of its decisions. Few of us stop to think who sets the rules for these tools or what safeguards are in place if something goes wrong. Yet, the policies shaping artificial intelligence (AI) impact every digital experience, affecting your choices, your rights, and your community's future.

AI policy refers to the laws, guidelines, and standards that govern the development, use, and monitoring of AI systems. At its heart, AI policy sets boundaries and responsibilities. Terms you'll often hear include:

- **AI regulation**: Official government rules directing or restricting specific AI uses, like bans on facial recognition in schools or rules for transparency in hiring systems.
- **Algorithmic transparency**: Making the workings of an AI understandable, rather than hiding it in a "black box."
- **Data privacy**: Protections ensuring your personal data—like

location, habits, or voice recordings—aren't collected, sold, or misused without consent.

- **Accountability**: Assigning responsibility if AI causes harm or is unfair.
- **Explainability**: The ability to get a clear, reasoned answer for why an AI chose a particular outcome that impacts you.

AI rules don't appear out of thin air. They result from negotiation among governments, tech companies, advocacy organizations, and citizens. In the European Union, the AI Act is landmark legislation requiring companies to demonstrate that their AI systems are safe and fair before release, covering areas from biometric surveillance to hiring, and imposing heavy obligations on businesses. The United States, by contrast, uses a more decentralized method, with federal agencies and states trying different guidelines rather than strict laws—often leaving much to company discretion. For example, the National League of Cities formed an AI Advisory Committee to help local leaders evaluate risks and opportunities of AI in city services or housing. Meanwhile, tech companies might make "self-regulation pledges" to audit their own products for bias or privacy risks—a move critics say often lacks real accountability.

These policy decisions reach into everyday life in unexpected ways. If your city uses an AI system to manage public housing waitlists, the algorithm may unintentionally favor some applicants. Without transparency or an appeal process, affected individuals have little recourse. Data protection laws like Europe's GDPR have pushed developers everywhere to improve privacy settings and let users control their data. At work, an AI scheduling tool could shift how assignments are made; if the system is not fair or explainable, it can lead to discrimination with no apparent reason given.

Policy debates center on challenging dilemmas, often making headlines or surfacing in public meetings. One core debate is between innovation and regulation. Those favoring looser rules warn that excessive regulation could stifle progress, slow health innovation, or dampen productivity. They highlight the surge in creative uses of AI across startups and research. But advocates for stronger rules caution that, without proper oversight, companies may overlook harms—especially for vulnerable groups. Another major dilemma is balancing privacy and public safety. Police may argue that facial recognition improves crime-solving and safety, yet privacy advocates warn about surveillance and wrongful identification. Cities take different approaches—some ban facial recognition in public spaces, while others allow it with strict oversight.

Reflection Exercise: Your Personal Stake in AI Policy

Take five minutes to list three ways AI already affects your daily life—at work, home, or in your community. Then consider: Who sets the rules for those technologies? Have you ever been able to request an explanation or challenge a software-made decision? Which rights—privacy, fairness, transparency—do you value most? Recognizing your personal stake reveals these policies are not just abstract concerns; they are practical matters of daily life and dignity.

As AI increasingly shapes society, debates over its governance will only grow. Whether as a voter, worker, parent, or someone invested in ensuring technology reflects shared values, your participation matters in shaping how this power is channeled and controlled.

JOINING THE CONVERSATION—HOW TO PARTICIPATE IN LOCAL TECH DECISIONS

You might not see yourself as a shaper of technology policy. Still, local decisions about AI—such as what schools adopt, which police tools cities use, or how libraries protect privacy—often take place in public forums. Your participation is not just welcome; it is needed. City council and school board meetings, typically streamed or open to the public, often include agenda items about tech adoption, and you do not need to be a specialist to make meaningful contributions. Simple questions like "How does this algorithm work?" or "How is user privacy protected?" can spark meaningful discussion and slow down hasty decisions that might not serve everyone well.

Public comment periods are another effective channel. When cities plan to implement AI-driven systems—such as traffic cameras, facial recognition, or student monitoring—they usually call for public feedback. These calls may be tucked away on websites or in newsletters, but submitting even a brief email with your concerns or support puts your perspective on record. For instance, in one case, residents' questions about bias in predictive policing led the city to pause and review its rollout.

Reaching out directly to local officials is also impactful. Crafting a clear, respectful message about your concerns or hopes for AI in government reminds policymakers that these issues matter to constituents. Here's a template you could use:

Dear [Councilmember/Mayor/Representative],

I am a resident of [neighborhood/city] writing with questions about the planned use of [name the AI system]. I am concerned about [privacy, fairness, transparency, or another issue] and would like to know what steps the city is taking to ensure equitable benefits. Thank you for your leadership, and I look forward to your response.

Sincerely,
[Your Name]
[Your Address or Neighborhood]

Most cities post agendas and contact details for representatives online.

Getting more involved can mean serving on advisory boards or committees. Recognizing the need for public input, cities often accept applications from residents—no technical background required—to participate on panels reviewing AI proposals, drafting guidelines, and representing community concerns. The application is usually straightforward, and your professional or personal experience can be highly valuable.

Public forums, hearings, or workshops offer another chance for advocacy. Events like "AI in Our Schools" nights enable parents, teachers, and students to discuss the introduction of new technology and address issues such as data handling and support for those struggling with adoption. Town halls on predictive policing or surveillance bring together residents and officials for open debate, providing a space to hear varied perspectives and raise your own in a collaborative environment.

If no event exists, consider organizing one yourself—partner with a local library, community center, or organization to host a forum on responsible AI. You need not be an expert—invite speakers or use resources from advocacy groups. Often, simply initiating the conversation can spark awareness and promote change.

Persistence is crucial. While one comment at a meeting might be missed, repeated questions—especially when echoed by others—can build momentum for transparency and accountability. Building alliances broadens your impact. Working with groups such as parent associations, neighborhood coalitions, civil rights organizations, or disability advocates increases influence and brings multiple perspectives to fair, safe tech use. For example, when planning surveillance in public parks, a group that included privacy advocates and youth organizations convinced the city to strengthen oversight and limit data retention.

Coalitions can also address less visible issues, such as algorithms for public housing waitlists. When residents found that single-parent households were being unfairly penalized, they combined their experiences and pressed the city council together. Their actions led to an independent audit and critical algorithm updates.

Change may be slow, and setbacks common, but sustained local engagement makes a difference. Small wins, such as delayed rollouts, required audits, or improved public reporting, can lead to broader reforms. Most importantly, recognize that your experiences and values deserve a place in these tech discussions. You don't need technical expertise to ask essential questions or demand fairness—your willingness to participate is a vital civic act.

BUILDING COMMUNITY—STARTING AN AI BOOK CLUB OR FORUM

Creating a space for open conversations about AI's impact on society can be straightforward and highly rewarding. Starting a book club, discussion group, or online forum centered on AI helps deepen your understanding while allowing others to participate and learn. You can choose a format that works best for your group—some prefer the consistency of in-person monthly meetings at a café or library. In contrast, others like the flexibility of online video calls or chat groups that span different schedules and time zones. Hybrid models are also effective, alternating between in-person and virtual meets as needed. No matter the format, prioritize an atmosphere where curiosity is valued and expertise is not a prerequisite.

Next, carefully curate your group's materials, as this will influence the club's tone and accessibility. Consider including a mix of books—memoirs by AI researchers, accessible scientific overviews, or essay collections from people directly affected by technology. To keep discussions relevant, include documentaries, podcasts, or recent news articles. Ensure diverse voices are represented; seek out work by women, people of color, and those outside traditional tech backgrounds. This not only expands perspectives but also ensures more participants feel a sense of belonging. Encourage everyone to suggest reading or viewing materials, allowing interests to shape the reading list.

When inviting others, use inclusive, clear language. For instance, you might say: "Interested in how AI is shaping our world? Join our book club to read, watch, and discuss the real-life impact of artificial intelligence—no technical experience required. All are welcome." Share invitations on community boards and online platforms, or reach out directly to colleagues and neighbors who might be interested.

Organize your meetings for engagement and preparation. Start with an icebreaker—perhaps sharing ways AI impacted members lately or discussing an interesting news item. Then guide the main conversation with open-ended prompts such as "What challenged your thinking?" or "Did something you learned shift your habits?" Foster an environment that welcomes personal reflections or questions without judgment. Wrap up each meeting by collaboratively choosing the next topic or resource, ensuring everyone has input in the group's direction.

Leadership within the group should be shared. Rotate discussion leaders each session to keep perspectives fresh and allow quieter members opportunities to facilitate. Send out a simple agenda in advance to help hosts prepare, but keep the structure flexible. If discussions get tense, refer back to the group agreements—listen respectfully, refrain from interruptions, and assume positive intent. If certain voices dominate, gentle reminders and structured sharing (like round robins) can ensure balanced participation. In online sessions, encourage contributions through chat for those who prefer writing over speaking. After meetings, check in privately with new members to gauge their experience and gather suggestions for improving inclusivity.

Consciously fostering inclusivity is essential. Set early norms emphasizing that all backgrounds are welcome and that curious, respectful disagreement is healthy. Use techniques like giving everyone a turn before moving to open discussion to surface quieter voices. Invite written input online for those who are less comfortable speaking up. Regular feedback—especially from new or marginalized members—helps continually refine group accessibility.

The impacts of these groups often extend beyond a single meeting. For example, a lunchtime reading group at one workplace prompted management to reevaluate their use of automated hiring processes. In another setting, weekly discussions about AI ethics led to advocacy for more transparent digital monitoring policies. A neighborhood forum even inspired local media coverage, sparking civic engagement around new technology in schools.

Parents and educators have found success in forming AI-focused clubs tailored to families. One such group, started by three caregivers, expanded quickly. Their conversations about children's exposure to technology equipped them to engage school boards, leading to new policies on classroom tool reviews. These examples show that meaningful influence doesn't require technical expertise—just curiosity, care, and the initiative to create a welcoming space for dialogue.

Ultimately, the most crucial step is to show up: bring your questions, experiences, and a willingness to listen. Over time, you'll see growing confidence, new members joining, and increasingly rich conversations. Bringing people together—whether in a living room, breakroom, or online—doesn't just reshape how individuals view technology; it can subtly influence whole communities as they decide what kind of future they want to build.

CIVIC TECH IN ACTION—CASE STUDIES OF GRASSROOTS IMPACT

Across the country, people without technical backgrounds have stepped up to challenge, refine, and sometimes reshape how artificial intelligence is used in their communities. These efforts often go unnoticed but create significant ripple effects. In one city, residents realized that predictive policing software—built on historical crime data—was targeting certain blocks for increased patrols, reinforcing existing biases. A coalition of local organizers, faith leaders, and parents formed, drafted a public petition, and collected stories highlighting the consequences. Their open letter demanded suspension of the tool and called for a transparent review. Beyond collecting signatures, they held public teach-ins to explain algorithmic bias and its impact. Eventually, the city paused the program, allowed for a public audit, and invited outside experts to review the software's decision-making.

On a college campus, students discovered facial recognition cameras installed to "improve safety," with little warning. Concerns grew about privacy and misidentification risks, especially for students of color. Student leaders partnered with advocacy groups and the local ACLU, launched a campaign with flyers, a hashtag, and open forums, and sent a letter to university officials citing research on inaccuracies and free speech concerns. Hosting an informational night with digital ethics faculty broadened support. Persistent pressure led the administration to remove the cameras and instate a moratorium on facial recognition until a review involving student input could be completed.

Often, public campaigns begin with a single spark—a neighbor spotting drones, or someone questioning an algorithmic rent increase. In one city, parents noticed surveillance drones in public parks and organized a petition demanding that the town pause the program and hold a public hearing. Their efforts gained momentum on local radio, culminating in the council suspending drone use for further review.

In another case, tenants faced abrupt rent hikes from an algorithmic pricing tool. Instead of only protesting, they organized a public audit with help from a civic tech nonprofit, gathering data from renters and comparing it to the software's outcomes. Their findings revealed unfair increases in specific neighborhoods. Presenting these results at a city council meeting prompted officials to suspend the tool temporarily and seek expert advice.

Change rarely comes easily. Grassroots groups often face resistance, with authorities arguing that technology is objective or too complicated for public input. Campaigns may stall over legal obstacles or claims of proprietary secrets, and groups commonly need technical allies—data scientists or lawyers—to clarify complex code or contracts. Progress is usually incremental: a program pause, transparency commitment, or formation of a review committee. Yet, each step builds accountability, raises awareness, and lays the foundation for further action.

These movements use accessible tactics. Petitions and open letters demonstrate widespread support. Public campaigns, through meetings, social media, or news, spotlight issues that might otherwise go unnoticed. Transparent tech audits, while often complex, become feasible through partnerships with nonprofits or universities. Core elements are persistence, creativity, and willingness to collaborate. Groups like Code for America and Algorithmic Justice League provide toolkits, templates, and volunteers. If you're unsure where to begin, start small: observe a civic tech issue in your daily life—like an unfair grading algorithm or opaque budgeting app—document it, discuss with neighbors, and look for others who care.

Even the youngest voices can spark change. In one city, teenagers concerned about school surveillance started a digital rights club, researched risks, shared findings with parents and teachers, and spoke before the city council. Their message—"We deserve to feel safe without being watched"—helped prompt a citywide pause on facial recognition in schools.

Grassroots civic tech does not require coding skills or deep policy expertise—just commitment, willingness to learn, and courage to act. Each small action counts. Noticing flaws and organizing with others is often all it takes to create impact.

As this chapter concludes, remember: every community holds the seeds of change. Ordinary people—students, parents, workers—have challenged systems, shifted norms, and pushed AI toward greater accountability. Next, we move to the global stage to see how diverse voices internationally are helping define what staying human means in AI's age.

CHAPTER 10
GLOBAL PERSPECTIVES AND DIVERSE VOICES

HUMAN-AI COLLABORATION AROUND THE WORLD—STORIES FROM FIVE CONTINENTS

IMAGINE STANDING in a bustling market in Brazil at sunrise. The air holds a promise of rain, but the clouds are tricky, and the fields stretch beyond the horizon. Here, farmers use AI-powered weather prediction tools on their mobile phones. For years, unpredictable rainfall led to ruined crops and hungry families. Now, with algorithms analyzing satellite images and local climate data, these farmers receive not just forecasts, but planting advice tailored to their region and crop cycles. One farmer, Lucia, describes her routine: she checks her phone before deciding whether to sow or wait. The AI doesn't just save money; it helps her keep faith in her family's future. In this setting, resilience means adapting centuries-old practices with state-of-the-art technology, blending ancestral wisdom with digital insight to protect both the land and the community.

Shift your attention to an industrial workshop in Germany, where the precise movements of AI-driven robots join the hum of machinery. Here, safety and efficiency are paramount. Workers like Stefan have learned to collaborate with robotic arms that handle the most hazardous tasks—lifting heavy metals, welding, assembling delicate electronics. Instead of feeling replaced, Stefan describes how these systems act as partners. He supervises, troubleshoots, and steps in when the unexpected occurs. Injuries have dropped, morale has risen, and each day feels less like a battle against fatigue and more like a demonstration of human ingenuity working alongside tireless, responsive automation. In this factory, the value of partnership and oversight is impossible to ignore; humans make the final calls while machines tirelessly extend their reach.

In rural Kenya, healthcare teams face a daily flood of patients with limited time and resources. Nurses and community health workers rely on AI-powered triage tools running on tablets. These applications sort symptoms, flag urgent cases, and suggest possible diagnoses, all in Swahili and local dialects. Fatima, a nurse in a small clinic, explains how the AI directs her to focus on a mother with a feverish child rather than a minor scrape. The system's recommendations are not perfect, but they help her save precious minutes and lives. Local adaptation is essential here; the AI's creators worked closely with Kenyan clinicians to ensure the language, medical norms, and cultural references matched the realities on the ground. When the tool once misread a common herbal remedy as a dangerous symptom, a quick correction by local staff updated the database for everyone—demonstrating the irreplaceable value of human oversight.

In Japan's aging society, where care for elders is both a tradition and a mounting challenge, AI companions are becoming household fixtures. In a cozy Tokyo apartment, Mrs. Sato sits with her robotic companion, which helps her remember medication times and offers gentle reminders to call her daughter. The device speaks with subtle shifts in tone, drawing on thousands of recorded interactions with elderly users. Local engineers spent years refining these nuances, ensuring the AI respected Japanese customs of politeness and indirect communication. While some worry about technology replacing human warmth, Mrs. Sato describes her companion as a supplement—a talking calendar and gentle friend that keeps loneliness at bay without taking the place of real visits. Here, technology is woven into care by honoring dignity and culture.

Across the Pacific in Australia, indigenous artists are reimagining storytelling. A collective in Queensland uses generative AI not to overwrite tradition but to amplify it. Collaborating with computer scientists, these artists teach algorithms about Dreamtime narratives, songlines, and visual motifs unique to their culture. The AI suggests new variations on ancient patterns or helps translate oral stories into interactive digital art exhibits. Elder Uncle Jimmy insists on reviewing every output before it is shared—his approval is final. When the AI once combined motifs from two different clans in a way that would have been disrespectful, the artists stepped in, corrected the error, and taught the system about sacred boundaries. The result is not just new art but a renewed sense of ownership. The technology adapts to culture, not the other way around.

Local adaptation shapes every one of these stories. In India, developers create multilingual virtual assistants that understand Hindi, Tamil, and dozens of other tongues spoken at home. These assistants answer questions about crops, health, and schooling in language that feels familiar and respectful. In Southeast Asia, agricultural AI is customized to recognize smallholder farm patterns—tiny plots, mixed crops, shifting weather—so advice is beneficial, not just repackaged from distant corporate models.

Across these examples, you see efficiency sought where resources are thin, safety prioritized in high-risk workspaces, and cultural preservation held sacred where tradition runs deep. Challenges are not uniform—a German assembly line's needs differ from those of a Kenyan clinic or an Australian art studio. Yet, everywhere, the best outcomes arise when humans remain in the loop—reviewing, correcting, guiding—while AI handles complexity and scale.

Reflection: Recognizing Human-AI Partnerships in Your World

Pause for a moment and consider where in your own life or work you might witness—or even shape—collaboration between people and intelligent systems. Which values guide these interactions: Safety? Tradition? Efficiency? Creativity? Write for five minutes about one human strength you believe should never be automated. What role could you play in keeping that value alive as technology advances?

LESSONS FROM THE GLOBAL SOUTH—INNOVATIVE USES OF AI FOR SOCIAL GOOD

In the humid lowlands of Ghana, malaria remains a daily threat, with outbreaks often overwhelming rural clinics and health workers. Here, AI-enabled disease surveillance has begun to shift the balance. Health officials collaborate with local hospitals and international researchers, feeding real-time patient data and weather patterns into machine learning systems. These tools spot early warning signs, flagging villages at risk before an outbreak spirals out of control. Nurses receive alerts by text message, sometimes days before symptoms become widespread. The difference this makes is not abstract—it means a mother can get her child to a clinic in time, and supplies can be sent before shelves run empty. This approach costs far less than traditional surveillance and works with patchy infrastructure, relying on basic mobile phones more than expensive computers.

In Jordan, refugees facing legal uncertainty often lack access to lawyers, resources, or even information in their own language. Community organizations, partnering with local technologists, have rolled out chatbots that provide basic legal aid. These chatbots answer questions in Arabic and English, guiding people through asylum paperwork or helping them understand their rights in unfamiliar systems. The solutions are simple—no flashy graphics, just clear, direct dialogue and resources available around the clock. For a young mother in a crowded camp, this means answers are just a text away, not a two-hour bus ride. Volunteers constantly refine the chatbot's knowledge base, adding new scenarios and clarifying answers as laws and policies shift.

Typhoons and floods batter the Philippines every year, leaving destruction that can take months to repair. Communities, government agencies, and universities partner to deploy AI-driven mapping tools that track storm movement, predict flood zones, and coordinate emergency response. Drones and satellites feed data to algorithms that generate up-to-the-minute risk maps. Local radio stations receive this information and broadcast alerts in multiple dialects, giving villagers time to evacuate or secure their homes. This system emerged from necessity—

after years of slow disaster response, local engineers and students built open-source tools tailored for the islands' unique geography and communication needs. Their work now helps save lives and minimize loss on a scale previously out of reach.

Resourcefulness defines innovation in these contexts. In places where smartphones are rare or internet access is unreliable, SMS-based AI tools connect farmers to weather updates, market prices, or pest alerts. A simple text—received on a basic handset—can mean the difference between profit and loss for a smallholder farmer. In Tanzania, an agricultural cooperative rolled out a system that allowed members to text crop-related questions to an AI-powered platform. The answers came back in Swahili, often within minutes. The simplicity of the tool is its strength; it works anywhere there is a signal, no app download required. Similarly, community radio stations in Madagascar and Nepal have begun integrating AI to curate hyper-local weather forecasts and health messages. The AI sifts through government bulletins, satellite feeds, and even listener call-ins, turning scattered data into relevant news. These broadcasts reach thousands who might never use a computer but rely on the radio for daily information.

The backbone of these efforts is partnership. UNICEF's AI initiatives in sub-Saharan Africa illustrate what's possible when local governments, grassroots organizations, and global tech companies work together. In several countries, UNICEF supports the development of AI-powered educational platforms that adapt to students' needs and languages. Teachers and students help shape lesson content, providing feedback that tunes the system for local realities—not just standardized test scores. Meanwhile, local NGOs team up with universities to offer AI literacy workshops. In Kenya and Rwanda, these workshops teach teenagers and adults how algorithms work, how to spot bias, and how to use AI for community projects. The focus is on empowerment, not just consumption; participants learn to shape technology rather than accept it.

These stories reveal that actual social impact comes from designing AI with communities, not just for them. Trust grows when people see themselves reflected in the technology—through language choices, content, and opportunities for feedback. Transparency is crucial; when villagers in Indonesia began using an AI platform for disaster alerts, the developers held town meetings, explained how the system made decisions, and invited suggestions. This openness built confidence and helped the tool evolve to meet local needs better. Community involvement keeps systems relevant, corrects errors quickly, and ensures no group is left out.

You may notice that even in places with few resources, people find ways to make technology work for them. The lesson is not about copying models from wealthier nations but about listening and learning from those who face the most rigid constraints. Their resilience and creativity show that AI can be a tool for empowerment even in the most challenging conditions. If you are thinking about social impact or considering how technology could serve your community, look to these examples. Engage those affected from the start. Insist on tools that are transparent and adaptable. When people feel ownership and understand how systems work, they use and improve them with pride, turning technology from an outside force into a shared asset.

BRIDGING THE DIGITAL DIVIDE—AI IN RURAL AND UNDERREPRESENTED COMMUNITIES

The digital divide is one of the most stubborn barriers in the age of artificial intelligence. It is the gap between those who can access and benefit from new technologies and those who cannot. This divide is not just about having a fast internet connection or the latest devices—it's about who gets opportunities, education, healthcare, and a voice in shaping the future. In many parts of rural Appalachia, for example, broadband access remains limited or patchy. Children do their homework in fast-food parking lots to use free Wi-Fi, and farmers cannot use innovative irrigation tools because their fields are out of network range. The divide is felt in language, too: countless indigenous tongues and dialects are missing from AI datasets, leaving millions cut off from voice assistants, translation tools, and automated services that work only in dominant languages. When AI does not speak your language, it cannot truly serve you.

Yet even in the face of these obstacles, people find ways to adapt and innovate. In remote northern stretches of Canada, where roads vanish and winter is long, clinics serving indigenous communities have adopted AI-powered telemedicine. A nurse might consult with a specialist hundreds of miles away, sending photos and patient data over low-bandwidth networks. The AI helps triage cases, flagging when an in-person visit is urgent or when symptoms can be managed locally. This system does not replace human care but supports it, making healthcare possible where it was once out of reach. In several African cities, community centers have become hubs for digital inclusion. Here, young people gather after school to use AI-powered language learning programs. Sometimes these run on donated laptops or even shared smartphones. The software adapts to each learner's pace and background, offering hope to children who might otherwise fall behind because of limited resources at home.

The hurdles blocking wider adoption of AI in these communities are often complex. Cost is an obvious one—new devices, software licenses, and reliable connectivity all add up. Infrastructure is another; without stable electricity or cell towers, even the best AI tool is useless. Cultural distrust can be just as powerful a barrier. For many, technology has been something done to them, not with them. Suspicion lingers over who controls these systems and whose interests they serve. In the face of all this, practical strategies have emerged that put power back in local hands. Tech hubs, often run by volunteers or small nonprofits, collect used computers, refurbish them, and offer training to anyone interested—students, elders, job seekers. These spaces become more than labs; they are gathering places where people share stories and skills. In some regions, "AI on wheels" brings digital education to villages. A van loaded with laptops and solar panels visits rural schools, offering workshops on basic coding, digital safety, and even AI literacy. These mobile labs bridge distance and spark excitement about learning, giving children and adults alike a rare chance to interact with new technology.

For those living far from major cities, the invitation to shape the digital future is rarely direct. Still, your actions can make a real difference. Volunteering with local digital literacy programs—whether teaching seniors to use smartphones or helping families set up secure email accounts—can transform someone's relationship with technology. If you work with language or culture, consider advocating for the inclusion of minority tongues in AI datasets. Push tech companies to recognize that voice assistants and translation tools should reflect the world's diversity, not flatten it. Donating your old laptop or tablet to a community tech initiative can extend its life and open doors for someone who cannot afford new equipment. Even small efforts add up, especially when paired with a spirit of listening and respect for local knowledge.

Think beyond just plugging in devices. True digital inclusion means asking whose needs are being met and who gets left out. It means supporting projects that empower people to create content in their own language or adapt existing tools to fit local customs. It means showing up for conversations about broadband expansion, digital rights, and ethical tech policy at town halls and school board meetings. If you notice that certain groups in your community are missing from technology training or decision-making, reach out and invite them in. Sometimes bridging the divide is as simple as sharing a ride to the library, pooling Wi-Fi in a church basement, or organizing a weekend "tech-a-thon" where neighbors learn together.

These acts of connection and advocacy ripple outward. They help build a world in which AI is not something reserved for big cities or wealthy families but a resource that supports health, education, and opportunity everywhere. When you support digital inclusion—even in small ways—you help ensure that artificial intelligence reflects not just a narrow slice of humanity but the full spectrum of our voices, skills, and dreams.

CULTURAL CONTEXT—HOW DIFFERENT SOCIETIES SHAPE AND RESPOND TO AI

When you look closely at how artificial intelligence enters daily life across the globe, you find far more than technology at work. Societal values, beliefs, and histories profoundly shape not just how AI is used, but how it is welcomed, questioned, or resisted. For example, attitudes toward privacy differ sharply between regions. In Scandinavia, there is a strong sense of collective trust and openness. Many people are comfortable sharing personal data with the state if it promises social benefits, such as better healthcare or more efficient public services. The logic is simple: if everyone participates, everyone benefits. Contrast this with the United States, where individualism and privacy are cherished. Americans often express anxiety about surveillance, even as they rely on private tech companies that gather massive amounts of personal information. This creates tension—people want convenience but fear losing control.

Japan brings another perspective, shaped by demographic realities and cultural narratives. With a rapidly aging population and a shrinking workforce, society has turned to robots and AI-driven companions not only to fill gaps in eldercare but to maintain a sense of dignity for older people. Many Japanese seniors welcome robot helpers; these companions are seen as extensions of family, not as threats. This openness is rooted in a long tradition of animism and respect for non-human agents, making the integration of AI into daily rituals more seamless than in cultures that view technology as cold or alien.

Governments and industries often design AI policies that reflect these distinct worldviews. China's centralized approach stands out—here, the government tightly controls AI development and deployment. Surveillance systems powered by facial recognition are widespread, justified as tools for maintaining public order. The state's role as a guardian is accepted in many quarters, though it sparks concern about personal freedoms. By contrast, the European Union has chosen a different path, placing privacy and algorithmic transparency at the center of regulation. The General Data Protection Regulation (GDPR) and new AI acts require companies to explain how algorithms work and to provide ways for citizens to challenge AI-driven decisions. This emphasis on rights and accountability is not just legal—it reflects a broader cultural belief in individual dignity and skepticism toward unchecked authority.

The stories societies tell themselves about AI also vary widely. In France, media coverage frequently frames AI as a tool for the common good. Debates focus on how to use technology to promote equality, improve social services, and protect vulnerable groups. This narrative is both pragmatic and idealistic, often cautioning against allowing private interests to dominate the conversation. Meanwhile, South Korean pop culture infuses AI into everyday life, from dramas about robot friends to advertisements for smart home devices. AI appears both as an exciting promise and as a companion woven into the fabric of urban living, reflecting a society comfortable with rapid change and innovation.

These differences are not abstract. They shape how you, wherever you live, come to understand what AI can and should do. They also influence whose voices are heard in global debates about ethics, safety, and opportunity. Sometimes, it is easy to assume that your own cultural assumptions—about privacy, autonomy, or progress—are universal. In reality, they are just one thread in a much larger tapestry.

It is worth pausing to ask yourself: How does my own background shape my hopes and worries about technology? Maybe you grew up in a community that values transparency above all, or perhaps you learned to be cautious in sharing personal details online. These instincts matter. They influence which products feel trustworthy, which policies you support, and how you interpret news about AI breakthroughs or failures. If you are curious to expand your perspective, try joining international forums or following news sources from outside your own country. The simple act of listening to global voices can reveal blind spots and open up new questions you may not have considered.

The landscape of AI is not flat. It is textured by centuries of belief, struggle, and adaptation. Some societies race ahead, eager to automate, while others ask hard questions about fairness and belonging. The global conversation is richer for this diversity. When you pay attention to these differences—not just in headlines, but in daily choices and national priorities—you become more prepared to think critically and compassionately about how AI should serve humanity.

Brief Ending to the Chapter

As this chapter closes, keep in mind that AI is not just built from code; people, stories, and values shape it. Looking beyond your own context helps you see both the possibilities and responsibilities that come with powerful technology. In the next chapter, we will turn these insights into concrete actions for building a more just and human-centered future.

CHAPTER 11
SEPARATING FACT FROM FICTION
DEBUNKING AI MYTHS

TOP 10 AI MYTHS—WHAT'S TRUE, WHAT'S NOT

AT GATHERINGS OR IN HEADLINES, sweeping claims about AI—like "AI will soon run the world" or "machines are smarter than people"—spark anxiety or awe. Sorting myth from reality can feel overwhelming. The truth: AI is a tool, not a magical entity or threat.

Let's start with the big myth: "AI will soon become conscious and take over the world." This narrative thrives in movies and media, implying machines will "wake up" and act on their own. In reality, today's AI systems lack self-awareness, intention, and feelings. They cannot desire or plot; even the best models are just sophisticated pattern matchers. As Yann LeCun emphasizes, "machines have no drives or desires." If you hear claims about AI "rebelling," ask for evidence beyond fiction.

Another myth: "AI will replace all human jobs." While AI automates some tasks—like data sorting and scheduling—entire jobs don't vanish overnight. Roles adapt. For example, after ATMs were introduced, bank tellers shifted to customer-focused work. Skills like creativity, empathy, and judgment remain in demand. So if someone claims mass replacement, ask which tasks will change and what new opportunities might arise.

A third misconception: "AI is always objective and unbiased." AI systems learn from data, which can reflect the biases of their creators. If the input data is flawed, so are the outputs. Timnit Gebru, a leading AI ethicist, has highlighted how facial recognition can misidentify and cause real harm. No algorithm is immune to human error or bias—question any claims of "neutral" AI.

Some think, "If an AI beats a human at chess, it's smarter in every way." Not so—AI is strong in specific domains, like chess, not in general reasoning. For instance, a chess engine can't fold laundry or interpret jokes. "AI today is very narrow," says Fei-Fei Li. Don't confuse expertise in one area with broad intelligence.

Another false belief: "You need to be a programmer to understand or use AI." Most people interact with AI daily—via search engines, recommendations, or navigation—without writing code. Understanding AI's impact doesn't require technical skills, just curiosity. Seek out plain-language resources for clarity.

It's also wrong to assume "all AI systems are created equal." AI comes in many forms: simple spam filters to complex language models. Each system has its own purpose, design, and data. Knowing what you're dealing with helps set realistic expectations.

Predictions like "AI can perfectly predict your behavior" are exaggerated. While companies use AI to guess what you might buy or watch, these are only probabilities and often miss. Algorithms can't anticipate every human choice—look for both their correct predictions and their mistakes.

One popular myth: "AI has common sense." While AIs might answer simple questions or write fluent text, they lack the background knowledge and adaptable reasoning that humans use daily. Chatbots making nonsensical suggestions or navigation apps giving unsafe directions show how AI falters where common sense is needed.

Believing "AI always knows the right answer" is risky. AI can process large amounts of data quickly, but it can make errors, especially in unfamiliar situations or with insufficient input data. Critical decisions

—like hiring or healthcare—need human oversight to catch and correct these mistakes.

Lastly, "AI will inevitably lead to dystopia or utopia." Some fear a world of surveillance and lost jobs; others imagine endless abundance. The outcome depends on our choices—how we design, regulate, and use AI. Technology forces us to define our values, as Sherry Turkle notes. Constantly scrutinize extreme claims—look for balanced evidence.

Myth vs. Reality: Quick Reference Table

MythRealityAI will soon become conscious and take over the world, according to evidence; current AI lacks self-awareness or intent and cannot replace all human jobs. Most jobs evolve; human skills remain crucial is always objective and unbiasedAI reflects human choices and data; bias is commonIf AI beats a human at chess, it's smarter in every wayAI excels in narrow tasks; can't generalizeYou need to be a programmer to understand or use AIEveryday users benefit from AI without codingAll AI systems are created equalAIs differ widely in complexity and purposeAI can perfectly predict your behaviorPredictions are statistical; mistakes are frequentAI has common senseLacks flexible reasoning and background knowledgeAI always knows the right answerProne to error; requires human oversightAI will inevitably lead to dystopia or utopiaOutcomes depend on choices we make—nothing is predetermined.

As you hear bold AI claims—whether utopian or dystopian—pause and ask: What's the evidence? Who gains from this narrative? Ground your understanding in facts, not hype, to keep your agency and insights strong.

SPOTTING DEEPFAKES AND MISINFORMATION—A PRACTICAL GUIDE

Imagine scrolling through your feed and encountering a video of a politician making outrageous claims or a celebrity in a bizarre situation. It's increasingly complex to trust what we see and hear online—welcome to the age of deepfakes. These synthetic media, crafted by AI, mimic real people's voices, faces, and movements with frightening accuracy. Deepfakes go far beyond basic digital tricks; they challenge our sense of reality and can be profoundly misleading. By using layered neural networks trained on thousands of faces or voices, deepfakes create convincing but fabricated content. Unlike simple edits or "cheapfakes" that slow down footage or splice scenes, deepfakes manipulate subtle expressions, blend voices, and sync lips so skillfully that most viewers barely notice the fakery. The stakes are high: deepfakes can distort elections, erode public trust, and damage reputations. The main difference from simple media manipulation is the level of sophistication and intent. While basic fakes might crop or subtitle out of context, deepfakes can fabricate entire interviews or endorsements, fooling even trained viewers and making awareness and detection crucial.

Knowing how to spot and verify dubious media is an essential skill. Whenever you encounter a suspicious video or audio clip, pause and investigate before acting on or sharing it. A good starting point is reverse image search—tools like Google Images or TinEye can help you see if a still from the video or image appears elsewhere. If you find the face or scene in another, unrelated context or much older posts, that's a red flag. Utilize trusted verification tools: Snopes debunks viral hoaxes, and browser extensions like InVID break videos down into frames for closer inspection. Look for physical clues. Deepfakes sometimes get blinking patterns wrong—humans blink unpredictably, but fakes may blink at uniform intervals or not at all. Lighting errors are also telling—look for shadows or reflections that don't match up naturally. Watch for mismatched lip movements and audio—if the speech doesn't sync or feels detached, it might be fake. Trust your instincts; if anything seems odd, take a closer look.

Deepfakes have already created substantial chaos. During recent elections, altered videos of politicians spread rapidly, disrupting debates and influencing voter opinion. For example, fabricated clips might put damaging statements into candidates' mouths, sway undecided voters, or fuel conspiracy theories. Similarly, celebrity deepfakes went viral, resulting in reputational harm or harassment. These fakes aren't just pranks; they've been used for blackmail, revenge, and inciting violence. On a personal level, they can manipulate private conversations or images to mislead families or employers. Even after exposure, the initial impression lingers, causing confusion and eroding trust. Serious consequences follow when people act on lies or when public figures must defend themselves over fabricated actions.

You can play a significant role in curbing misinformation. Social platforms like YouTube, Facebook, and X (formerly Twitter) offer the option to report suspicious content. Reporting might feel minor, but collective action helps platforms improve their detection and reduces the spread of deceptive media. In your own circles, such as family or community groups, share accurate corrections by offering context instead of just saying "that's fake." For example: "This clip was flagged by fact-checkers as manipulated—here's more information." Avoid shaming those who share misinformation—most don't realize it's deceptive. Encourage skepticism: pause before sharing anything that sparks strong emotion or feels perfectly tailored to your perspective. A good practice is to treat viral content as a rumor—always verify before passing it on.

Interactive Element: Deepfake Detection Checklist

Before believing or sharing a viral image or video, ask yourself:

- Does the face blink naturally and at irregular intervals?
- Are lighting and shadows consistent across the entire scene?
- Is lip and speech synchronization believable?
- Have you run a reverse image search to check for earlier appearances?
- Are reputable news or fact-checking outlets discussing or debunking the clip?

- Does the content try to provoke a strong emotional response or outrage?
- Have you checked analysis sites like Snopes or InVID?

In our digital age, trust is based on healthy skepticism and smart habits. By pausing, verifying, and constructively engaging, you can slow the spread of misinformation and help keep your community informed and secure.

CHALLENGING TECH UTOPIANISM AND DYSTOPIANISM

It's easy to find yourself drawn to extremes when thinking about artificial intelligence. On one side, some believe AI will fix every problem—ending poverty, curing diseases, and even bringing about world peace. This is tech utopianism, the belief that technology is the ultimate answer, capable of ushering in a golden age in which social ills disappear. Utopian thinking promises a future where algorithms run fairly, machines work tirelessly for us, and everyone prospers thanks to digital innovation. On the other side, tech dystopianism paints a much darker picture. This view insists that AI will overrun jobs, wreck democracy, and unravel the fabric of human life. The dystopian narrative is full of fear: faceless machines replacing workers, governments tracking every move, or humanity losing control to the very tools we built. Both extremes—believing AI will save us or destroy us—miss the complicated reality and make it harder for us to have clear, productive conversations.

People are naturally drawn to black-and-white thinking, especially in times of uncertainty. When faced with something as complex and fast-moving as AI, it's tempting to take refuge in sweeping narratives. Fear of the unknown is a powerful force. Uncertainty can make anyone anxious, and the future of technology seems especially unpredictable. Utopian stories offer comfort, a sense of order, and the hope that someone (or something) will sort out our messes. Dystopian tales let us give in to anxiety, preparing for the worst so that we won't be caught off guard. Both stem from the same desire for control when life feels overwhelming. Media coverage amplifies these tendencies. Headlines often celebrate AI breakthroughs as triumphs of human achievement or warn of dire consequences if things go wrong. Sensationalism grabs your attention and keeps you glued to the story, but it rarely leaves room for honest doubt or pragmatic thinking. Social media piles on, promoting the most engaging—often extreme—takes rather than nuanced discussion. When everyone around you seems to be picking sides, it can feel risky to ask questions or look for middle ground.

What gets lost in these extremes is the reality that AI, like all technologies, is both powerful and limited, promising and risky. It's neither a savior nor a villain. The truth is that AI can be a force for good—improving healthcare, making work safer, or expanding educational access—while also creating new challenges, including bias, surveillance, and job shifts. The future is contingent, not inevitable. AI's impact depends on how people design, regulate, and use these tools. Productive thinking about AI means holding two ideas at once: technology can be both beneficial and risky. This "both/and" mindset is not wishy-washy; it's realistic. You can be excited about AI's potential to help doctors diagnose illnesses faster while still worrying about privacy and bias in medical data. If someone claims there's only one path ahead—whether it's utopia or disaster—pause. Ask who benefits from that view and what evidence supports it.

History shows that every major technology has brought both progress and disruption. The printing press once sparked fears about moral decay and loss of authority, yet it also gave rise to democracy and literacy. The industrial revolution replaced some jobs and created others, fueling both social upheaval and new opportunities. Electricity transformed cities and homes, but only after bitter fights over safety and access. Each wave of innovation brought new dangers and new possibilities, shaped by the choices people made along the way. AI is no different: it is a tool that reveals our values, not an unstoppable force with its own agenda. Looking at the past reminds us that it's possible to steer technological change toward more humane outcomes—if we stay curious, skeptical, and involved.

Balanced voices are steering the AI debate away from extremes and toward practical solutions. Sherry Turkle, a psychologist and technology scholar, has long urged us to use technology as a tool for connection, not a substitute for genuine relationships. Kate Crawford, an expert in AI ethics, calls for transparency and accountability rather than unchecked optimism or paranoia. Organizations like Partnership on AI bring together engineers, ethicists, and community leaders to hammer out guidelines for responsible development. Data & Society works to ensure that debates about algorithms include not just technical experts but also ordinary people affected by these systems. These groups champion policies that promote fairness, openness, and shared responsibility. They don't ignore risks or promise miracles; instead, they invite everyone—including you—to participate in shaping what comes next. These pragmatic voices recognize that real progress happens through thoughtful debate, experimentation, and a willingness to learn from mistakes.

You don't have to choose between hope and fear. The most productive stance is to remain open to possibilities but alert to risk. Ask where a claim comes from, who stands to gain or lose, and how new technologies fit into the bigger picture of human life. Remember that AI is made by people—and can be guided by people—if we remain engaged, honest, and willing to ask hard questions. This balanced approach keeps us alert to both dangers and opportunities, so we can help steer AI toward outcomes that align with our deepest values and needs.

BECOMING ALGORITHMICALLY LITERATE—EVERYDAY CRITICAL QUESTIONS

Algorithmic literacy involves recognizing how automated decisions—recommendations, rankings, or predictions—affect your daily life. This isn't just for software engineers or data scientists; everyone should develop this awareness, given how algorithms now influence what we see, buy, and believe. Whether a streaming service queues your next show, a hiring platform sorts résumés, or a health app nudges you with advice, these systems shape your attention and choices, sometimes subtly over time. Awareness is key: once you notice algorithmic influence, you can ask informed questions and better safeguard your interests.

Start by regularly questioning AI-powered systems. Ask: What data powers this tool, and who chooses that data? When you book a flight and see fluctuating prices, consider: Is this system tracking my location, browsing history, or device? If you get a recommendation from a shopping or streaming site, reflect on who benefits if you click or buy. Often, algorithms promote certain sellers, brands, or headlines—typically those with more influence or money.

Transparency is crucial. If you feel a decision—like a loan denial or job rejection—is unfair, does the company explain its criteria? Can you discover the reasons behind outcomes or appeal them? Not all systems provide clear explanations, so look for transparency, and don't hesitate to ask directly for more details. Remember: algorithms are built by people, who sometimes make mistakes or overlook important factors.

Bias and Fairness

Bias can affect any automated process. When using systems that sort, recommend, or predict, ask yourself: Could this tool be excluding or unfairly treating certain groups? For instance, online job applications may filter out some résumés before human review. A health app might offer advice that doesn't align with your age, culture, or medical history. If you sense the results are skewed, it may be due to hidden biases in the data, logic, or the tool creators' goals. Always stay alert to who benefits and who might be disadvantaged.

Everyday Strategies

Consider practical scenarios: when booking travel, you may see different prices for the same seat depending on your browsing history, location, or device. Clear your cookies or use a different browser to check if prices change—small actions like this often reveal the personalization at work. If a job or loan application portal doesn't explain rejections or seems to filter certain groups, request to see the criteria and appeal process. With health apps, don't simply accept advice—verify that suggestions suit your background and check if you can review or update the data used for predictions.

Encouraging Literacy in Others

Algorithmic literacy is not just personal—it's social. Share your insights at work if your team adopts a new automated tool; ask about its selection and monitoring for fairness and accuracy. Foster an environment where questioning these systems is encouraged. If you have children in school, ask educators what data decision-making tools they use and whether parents can review or challenge the outcomes. In your community, raise transparency issues with advocacy groups or at meetings. The more people demand fairness and accountability, the greater the pressure on companies and agencies to improve.

Shaping the Future

Algorithmic systems are neither neutral nor fixed. Staying curious and vocal means helping to set higher standards for fairness and accountability, ensuring technology serves everyone, not just those who design it. This isn't about fear, but about cultivating an empowered, informed relationship with the digital world.

In sum, algorithmic literacy is now essential for navigating life. By questioning, sharing, and advocating, you become part of a broader movement directing technology's future. Hold on to these habits as technology evolves—they'll help you stay adaptive, aware, and truly human in an algorithm-guided world. Up next, we'll cover how to put this literacy into concrete action, building a future where technology and humanity advance together.

CHAPTER 12
TAKING ACTION
BUILDING YOUR HUMAN-CENTERED AI FUTURE

DESIGNING YOUR PERSONAL "AI AND HUMANITY" ACTION PLAN

IMAGINE RETURNING HOME after a long day. Your phone buzzes with a calendar alert, your child's homework is auto-edited by software, and your work emails include drafts by AI. Technology is woven into your routine, influencing how your day unfolds. Despite its seamless presence, you still have a say in which technologies should be enhanced, reduced, or left untouched. This chapter encourages you to pause and actively design a future where AI serves your most essential values.

Begin by identifying three core values that guide you in any context—at home, work, or in your community. For instance, empathy helps you connect genuinely with others, even when fast chatbot replies are available. Creativity can remind you to trust your gut and originality over generic AI solutions. Fairness drives you to seek equitable treatment from the technologies you use or recommend. Write these down, then match each value with a specific technology-related commitment. For example: "Empathy—when communicating with clients through AI, I'll add a personal note or follow up directly. Creativity—I'll test new AI tools but trust my instincts. Fairness—I'll request explanations for algorithmic decisions and question their fairness."

From these values, set two or three practical, measurable goals for integrating ethical AI into your day-to-day life. You could pledge: "I'll review privacy settings on all my family's devices this month." Or, "Each week, I'll spend an hour device-free with loved ones." In the workplace: "Before adopting an AI tool, I'll ask about its transparency and bias controls." Concrete, achievable goals increase your likelihood of success—think of these as promises to yourself and those around you.

Break each goal into small, weekly steps. Significant changes last only if built from manageable actions. Hoping to increase empathy at home? This week, do a five-minute screen-free "highs and lows" check-in with each family member. Want fairness at work? Spend ten minutes hearing a colleague's experience with a new AI system. For creativity, try brainstorming with an AI assistant, but review outcomes yourself. These small actions build habits that support your values and allow for ongoing reflection and improvement.

Interactive Template: Personalizing Your Action Plan

Use this template to make your plan specific and actionable:

In my role as [teacher/parent/healthcare worker/small business owner], I will...

- Value 1: ____________
- Action: "I will [describe a specific way you'll express this value with technology]."
- Value 2: ____________
- Action: "I will [describe another concrete step]."
- Value 3: ____________
- Action: "I will [describe a third action]."
- Weekly Micro-Action: "Each [Monday/Friday/after dinner], I will [insert an easy, repeatable step supporting these values]."

Examples:

- Teacher: "I'll use AI for grading quizzes but give individual feedback on projects. Each week, I'll check in with a student about how technology affects their learning."
- Small Business Owner: "I'll review AI recommendations but consult my team before adopting new tools. Every Friday, I'll ask for feedback on tech's impact on fairness and workload."
- Healthcare Worker: "I'll use AI to schedule, but always ensure patients' unique needs are considered. Each week, I'll review one case where human judgment was key."
- Parent: "I'll use parental controls and talk with my child about technology's impact on their feelings. Every Sunday, we'll have a screen-free family activity."

Perfection isn't required. Obstacles will arise—motivation may decrease, distractions may appear, and old habits might return. When this happens, revisit your values and remember your initial motivation. Use reminders—like sticky notes, calendar alerts, or a bracelet. Find an "AI action buddy"—a friend, partner, or colleague who shares your goals, and check in weekly to share progress and setbacks. Accountability is there for support, not guilt.

If you slip up, acknowledge it without self-criticism and start fresh. Progress isn't always linear. Celebrate your wins, even small ones.

Envision a day when technology amplifies your core values instead of undermining them. See yourself making AI-powered choices with discernment, prioritizing real connection, and advocating for fairness. Picture your family, team, or community benefiting from your thoughtful use of technology. Affirm to yourself: "I am the author of my digital life."

INSTANT-IMPACT "RED FLAG" SPOTTER—QUICK REFERENCE FOR DAILY LIFE

Navigating the world of AI means regularly facing hidden risks behind appealing tech. Most adults encounter new tools or apps weekly—at work, home, or through their children—yet many struggle to distinguish between safe, fair technology and questionable or harmful options. That's why you need a fast, practical method to pause, assess, and protect yourself and loved ones. Enter the "Five-Second Red Flag Rule," a portable checklist for any situation—downloading a health app, signing up for a smart device, or letting your child use an AI-powered toy. Save it on your phone, print it for your wallet, or keep it near your workspace.

Here's how it works: When you meet a new AI tool, ask yourself these five yes/no questions—quickly and honestly.

1. Does the tool clearly explain what it does and why in plain language?
2. Can you see what data it collects and how it is used or stored?
3. Is there a way to appeal or contest its decisions, or is it a black box?
4. Do you know who is responsible if it makes a mistake—can you contact a human?
5. Has the tool or company faced complaints about bias, privacy, or fairness, and are these concerns addressed?

A "no" to any question is a red flag—pause and proceed with caution.

Examples

Imagine applying for a job using an automated hiring platform that provides no clear info on how resumes are filtered, offers no human review, and lacks a visible privacy statement. These are three immediate red flags: lack of transparency, no recourse, and ambiguity on data use. Take a screenshot, note the site, and contact the employer for details. Silence or resistance suggests you should carefully reconsider or seek alternatives.

Or, consider buying an innovative toy for your child. The packaging advertises AI features, but privacy details are buried, and you can't control data sharing. The lack of clear explanation and murky data policies are red flags. Check reviews from other parents, search for news on security, or contact the company. Sometimes, the best option is to walk away and find something more reliable.

Health apps pose similar risks. You download a fitness tracker promising personalized insights, but find only vague privacy terms and no info on how your data is used. Glowing testimonials can't replace transparency. Before sharing personal information, look up independent reviews and compare privacy standards. If red flags build up, seek better alternatives.

What To Do When You Spot a Red Flag

If you notice a red flag, pause. Gather more information: read user reviews, look for press coverage of complaints, or check watchdog sites for ratings. If serious concerns arise, report the app or device to consumer protection agencies, your company's tech team, or a digital safety hotline. Public feedback can prompt companies to respond and improve.

Spreading the Red Flag Spotter

Share this tool with others—text the checklist to friends or family, bring it up in group chats, or discuss it at family meetings. At work, offer to lead a quick discussion on digital safety and walk colleagues through the checklist using their favorite apps. For broader impact, post on social media to raise awareness and encourage those you know to use the checklist before trusting a new tool. These conversations help others build their confidence and caution in digital spaces.

Making It Practical

Create a "Red Flag Card"—write the five questions on an index card and keep it handy by your computer or in your bag. Take a photo for quick access when making digital choices. With practice, using this checklist becomes second nature, helping you spot patterns that separate trustworthy technology from risky options.

Setting an Example

Using and sharing the checklist models good habits for others. Kids notice when adults pause before clicking "agree," and coworkers appreciate seeing thoughtful questions about new tools. Even one person using the red flag rule can influence a culture toward safer, fairer tech use. If the checklist has helped you, share your story—through conversation, emails, or posts. Your experience can prompt others to think twice and stay protected.

JOINING THE MOVEMENT—HOW TO CONNECT WITH LIKE-MINDED CHANGEMAKERS

You do not have to chart a course through the AI landscape alone. In fact, you are surrounded by others who share your concerns, questions, and hopes for a more human-centered technological future. Many people, like you, want to see AI strengthen the community, uphold fairness, and protect what is deeply human. Yet, it can feel intimidating to seek out these connections, especially if you consider yourself an "ordinary" user rather than a tech expert. The truth is, some of the most meaningful progress comes from individuals who care and choose to act together.

You can find many welcoming networks and organizations devoted to ethical and inclusive AI. The Algorithmic Justice League stands out for its commitment to exposing and addressing AI bias, especially in facial recognition and hiring systems. Their online community provides resources, regular updates, and ways to report concerns or share experiences. Data for Black Lives brings together activists, scholars, and technologists to challenge bias and discrimination, focusing on how algorithms impact marginalized communities. Tech for Good chapters exist in cities around the world, hosting lively meetups—both in person and online—where people gather to discuss real-world AI dilemmas and solutions. If you prefer virtual spaces, many like-minded groups meet on Slack or Discord, where you can join conversations about digital well-being, responsible design, and equity in tech. Online forums such as the Partnership on AI and the Digital Wellness

Collective invite members to collaborate on projects or offer support and advice.

If you are more comfortable starting local, look for meetups on platforms like Meetup.com using keywords such as "AI ethics," "digital well-being," or "tech and society." Many libraries and community centers host book clubs or speaker nights focused on technology's impact—these events attract a mix of newcomers and seasoned advocates. If nothing exists nearby, you can create your own group with minimal effort. Pick a public place, choose a discussion topic or article (perhaps from one of the organizations above), and invite neighbors or colleagues. Often, curiosity alone is enough to draw a small group willing to talk about what technology means for your community or family.

Time constraints or lack of expertise should not stop you from getting involved. Many groups welcome "drop-in" participation—join when your schedule allows, listen in, and contribute only if you wish. Online discussions and virtual workshops mean you can participate from home after the kids are asleep or during a lunch break at work. Many movements host community challenges: for example, a week-long "digital detox" with daily prompts, or collaborative projects to translate AI safety guidelines into local languages. You can add your voice to public comment periods on tech regulations—these opportunities often appear on city or school district websites and ask for short comments, not technical essays. Even if you have just five minutes, you can make an impact by sharing your lived experience or concerns.

Stories from readers show how small steps build belonging and influence. Consider the parent who joined a school board's technology committee after noticing her child's class relied on automated grading. She admitted her nerves at the first meeting, but soon found her perspective valued by teachers and administrators. She helped shape a policy that now requires human review of AI-generated grades. Another example comes from a young professional who volunteered at a nonprofit teaching digital literacy to adults. She started by helping with workshops on privacy basics and soon became a trusted mentor for families navigating school and health apps. A community group in a multilingual neighborhood worked together to translate AI-powered public service tools into minority languages, making vital resources accessible to neighbors who had previously been excluded. Their success inspired other cities to adopt similar models.

You can amplify your impact by inviting someone to join you. Bringing a friend, colleague, or family member doubles your confidence and broadens the pool of ideas. If you want to reach out, try a simple invitation: "I found this event about ethical technology—would you like to join me? I think your experience would add something special." Or suggest hosting a "tech and humanity" lunch-and-learn at work—bring snacks, pick an article or podcast episode, and discuss how digital changes affect your team. Even a small gathering can spark bigger changes by making technology's impact visible and actionable.

With every new connection you make, you strengthen the movement for responsible and inclusive technology. Your perspective matters—and when combined with others' energy and insight, it gains power. Whether you join an established organization, participate in a one-time workshop, or invite a friend to reflect with you over coffee, you become part of a growing network working to restore the human heartbeat in the age of machines.

YOUR AI FUTURE JOURNAL—REFLECTION PROMPTS FOR LIFELONG GROWTH

Journaling is more than recording thoughts; it's a powerful tool for understanding, growth, and fostering accountability in your relationship with technology. Psychological research shows that writing about experiences can help rewire your brain, making sense of change and solidifying new habits. Reflecting is not just observation—it's active engagement, shaping how you interact with technology, one journal entry at a time. A simple notebook can guide you through uncertainty. In a world of ever-increasing screens and quick decisions, taking a moment to slow down and write offers clarity and intention. Starting an "AI and Humanity" journal doesn't require fancy supplies or perfect grammar—just a willingness to pause and notice what technology evokes in you.

Set aside ten minutes at the end of each day or week. Find a quiet spot, open a blank page, and be curious. Ask yourself: What moment today did technology help me connect with someone? Maybe it was a video call bridging miles or a shared playlist that sparked laughter. Next, consider where an AI tool influenced your decisions. Did you follow a map app's directions without question, or accept an algorithm's suggestion even when it didn't quite fit? Write about your feelings and actions in those moments. These reflections are clues about where AI is supporting or steering your life.

Each week, notice surprises in your emotional responses. Did a chatbot frustrate or comfort you unexpectedly? Did you feel gratitude for a digital assistant or unease when something felt off? These reactions reveal deeper patterns in your values and needs. Ask challenging questions—how have you used your voice in standing up for fairness or empathy? Did you raise concerns about bias at work? Did you help a family member set device boundaries? Record these moments, however small—they're the building blocks of mindful engagement.

Your journal can take many forms: handwriting, digital notes, or voice memos. If short on time, try a weekly summary page; jot down highlights, challenges, and questions. For more structure, use a "three highs and three lows" format, adding a note on how AI impacted each. If your schedule is packed, record brief voice memos during your commute or walk. The format is less important than your commitment to return regularly to your reflections.

To see your growth, review your journal each month. Ask yourself, "What's changing in my habits or perspective?" Identify fading old patterns and emerging new ones. Celebrate progress, even the most minor shifts. Once a year, write a letter to your future self about your AI relationship. What do you want to keep, change, or let go of in the coming year? These letters serve as milestones, marking your agency and wisdom as it evolves.

This form of journaling is not about perfection, but about nurturing self-awareness as the world changes. Your feelings about technology are not set; they evolve with new experiences and conversations. Returning to your journal allows space for honesty, gentle correction, and celebration of your unique human perspective in an era shaped by machines.

As you look back at your notes, notice patterns—moments where AI amplified your values or clashed with them. These patterns inform future choices: what to keep, what to question, or where to push for change. Reflection reminds you that, even when technology feels overwhelming, you are still an active participant in your own story.

You may choose to share some insights with friends, family, or colleagues. Sometimes, reading your journal aloud can start meaningful conversations and raise awareness. Over time, your journal becomes both a record and a resource—a living document of how you adapt to and shape technology in your life.

As this chapter closes, remember: your reflections matter. Each moment of honesty and curiosity builds resilience and guides your next steps. These habits connect the personal with the collective, ensuring that our digital future makes space for what is most human. In upcoming chapters, we'll continue to explore how to stay steady and purposeful as technology evolves.

CONCLUSION

You and I have traveled a long and winding road together through these pages. At the heart of this journey lies a simple, unwavering truth: Staying human—rooted in compassion, wisdom, and purpose—is not only possible in the age of AI, but necessary. Technology should serve humanity, never replace it. My vision, which I hope now resonates with you, is that we can restore and protect the human heartbeat within our digital lives. Progress matters most when guided by our deepest values.

Let's pause to recall where we've been. We began by demystifying AI in your everyday life. We saw it in music playlists, intelligent assistants, social media feeds, and even in the classroom. You learned to spot where algorithms are already shaping your routines and choices. Next, we built AI fluency together. Using analogies, plain language, and everyday stories, we cut through jargon. We practiced critical reading, separated hype from reality, and made sense of "black boxes" that sometimes cloud technology's workings.

We then turned inward, focusing on the strengths only humans can bring: creativity, empathy, critical thinking, and moral judgment. You discovered how to use AI as a muse, not a master. You practiced active listening, mindful pauses, and ethical reflection. From there, we moved into the real world—applying practical frameworks for ethical AI. You learned how to identify red flags, ask tough questions, and demand transparency and fairness. We explored how to adapt your work and skills, nurture your well-being, and preserve authentic relationships in a world filled with digital distractions.

You learned to recognize and challenge bias, both in the tools you use and in the larger systems shaping our lives. We discussed ways to engage in local decisions, influence tech policy, and build community through conversation and action. Global voices and diverse stories reminded us that AI looks different everywhere, yet it meets the same human need for dignity, fairness, and meaning everywhere. Along the way, we debunked popular myths—reminding ourselves that AI is neither magic nor menace, but a tool shaped by human intentions.

Now, as you reach this final chapter, I hope you see how much you already hold. You know how to recognize AI's touch in your daily life. You have practical tools to evaluate the ethics and fairness of technology—whether it's a new app for your child, an algorithm at work, or an automated service in your community. You can nurture your unique human gifts, adapt your professional life, protect your attention, and foster genuine connection. You have scripts to speak up when something feels off, and checklists to help others do the same. You know how to keep learning, reflecting, and growing as technology changes.

I invite you to bring these insights into your real life—starting today. Perhaps you'll use the "Red Flag" checklist before downloading a new app. Maybe you'll set aside device-free time for conversation or ask your employer about transparency in AI-driven tools. You might help your child practice empathy by discussing how Alexa or Siri differs from a real friend. Or you'll join a local group, workplace discussion, or online forum to share what you've learned and learn from others. These aren't distant ideals—they are practical steps, ready for you to try.

Of course, the path ahead is neither smooth nor simple. Staying human with AI is ongoing work. It takes courage to question a system everyone else accepts. It demands humility to admit when you don't know, or when you must change your mind. Some days it will feel messy and uncertain, and that's normal. But you are not alone. Every mindful choice, every moment of reflection, every conversation about fairness and empathy adds up to real change. Collective action doesn't always make headlines, but it shapes the world in quiet, persistent ways.

So I urge you—become an active shaper of your digital life. Use the tools, checklists, stories, and reflection prompts from this book. Advocate for fairness, transparency, and kindness wherever technology touches your family, your workplace, or your community. Share what you learn. Invite others into the conversation. When you notice a gap or a harm, speak up—not only for yourself, but for those whose voices may go unheard.

Remember, AI will keep evolving. The questions you face today will be different tomorrow. That's why curiosity and lifelong learning matter. Revisit your action plan. Keep your "AI Future Journal." Stay open to new ideas, and return to your values as your compass. Adaptation is not a one-time event—it's a way of being.

Above all, I want to leave you with hope and a sense of agency. You have more power than you think. Our choices—personal and collective—will determine whether AI deepens our humanity or erodes it. As I've seen in my decades of listening to people's stories, even small acts of compassion and wisdom ripple outward. The future is not written in code alone; it is written in courage, friendship, fairness, and love.

So as you close this book, remember: Progress is not about moving faster, but about moving forward together—with heart, with integrity, and with purpose. As one wise voice said, "We shape our tools, and thereafter our tools shape us." Let's shape them wisely, so that the world we build with AI is one where everyone can thrive.

The next step is yours. Stay human, stay curious, and know that you are never alone in this work.

REFERENCES

- *Everyday examples and applications of artificial ...* https://www.tableau.com/data-insights/ai/examples
- *Everything You Need to Know About Social Media Algorithms* https://sproutsocial.com/insights/social-media-algorithms/
- *21 Ways People Are Using A.I. at Work* https://www.nytimes.com/interactive/2025/08/11/upshot/ai-jobs.html
- *What I learned from sharing my private self with an AI journal* https://psyche.co/ideas/what-i-learned-from-sharing-my-private-self-with-an-ai-journal
- *Learn AI Through 6 Analogies* https://medium.com/student-of-life/learn-ai-through-6-analogies-456c15ab1747
- *A Plain-Language Glossary of AI Terms for Editors* https://www.inkbotediting.com/blog/ai-terms-for-editors-glossary
- *How to Spot Fake News in the Age of AI* https://pac.org/impact/how-to-spot-fake-news-in-the-age-of-ai
- *Ten Stories of Black Box Model Failures* https://ishanjainoffical.medium.com/the-stories-of-black-box-model-failures-6f6dad58faa5
- *How AI Generative Models Are Transforming Creativity* https://www.forbes.com/councils/forbestechcouncil/2024/10/22/how-ai-generative-models-are-transforming-creativity-real-world-case-studies-in-art-music-and-writing/
- *How to Understand and Bridge the Empathy Gap ...* https://blog.heartmanity.com/empathy-gap
- *Critical Evaluation Frameworks for AI-Generated Content* https://stars.library.ucf.edu/teachwithai/2024/tuesday/9/
- *Artificial Intelligence: examples of ethical dilemmas* https://www.unesco.org/en/artificial-intelligence/recommendation-ethics/cases
- *Evaluating AI Tools - Artificial Intelligence at ...* https://it.purdue.edu/ai/evaluating-ai-tools/
- *Real-life Examples of Discriminating Artificial Intelligence* https://datatron.com/real-life-examples-of-discriminating-artificial-intelligence/
- *Exploring privacy issues in the age of AI* https://www.ibm.com/think/insights/ai-privacy
- *Case Studies - Princeton Dialogues on AI and Ethics* https://aiethics.princeton.edu/case-studies/
- *Beyond critical thinking: 13 durable skills driving AI adoption* https://www.multiverse.io/en-GB/blog/beyond-critical-thinking-13-durable-skills-driving-ai-adoption
- *How AI is poised to disrupt the job market* https://www.cnbc.com/2025/10/08/how-ai-is-poised-to-disrupt-the-job-market.html
- *How to Navigate AI Anxiety and Embrace Change in Your ...* https://

exenalearninghub.com/how-to-navigate-ai-anxiety-and-embrace-change-in-your-career/

- *AI for Everyone* https://www.deeplearning.ai/courses/ai-for-everyone/
- *AI Chatbots have shown they have an 'empathy gap' that ...* https://www.cam.ac.uk/research/news/ai-chatbots-have-shown-they-have-an-empathy-gap-that-children-are-likely-to-miss
- *Digital guidelines: Promoting healthy technology use for ...* https://www.apa.org/topics/social-media-internet/technology-use-children
- *Rising Use of AI in Schools Comes With Big Downsides for ...* https://www.edweek.org/technology/rising-use-of-ai-in-schools-comes-with-big-downsides-for-students/2025/10
- *Our Epidemic of Loneliness and Isolation* https://www.hhs.gov/sites/default/files/surgeon-general-social-connection-advisory.pdf
- *A Comprehensive Review on Digital Detox* https://pmc.ncbi.nlm.nih.gov/articles/PMC11109987/
- *Human-in-the-Loop: An Intersection of People and ...* https://execsintheknow.com/magazines/april-2024-issue/human-in-the-loop-an-intersection-of-people-and-technology/
- *AI and Digital Distraction: Impact of Smart Technologies on ...* https://www.researchgate.net/publication/393061956_AI_and_Digital_Distraction_Impact_of_Smart_Technologies_on_Time_and_Health_Management_Article_Details_ABSTRACT
- *Fostering Digital Well-Being Through (e-)Service-Learning* https://pmc.ncbi.nlm.nih.gov/articles/PMC12466529/
- *What Is Algorithmic Bias?* https://www.ibm.com/think/topics/algorithmic-bias
- *Measuring Fairness - People + AI Research* https://pair.withgoogle.com/explorables/measuring-fairness/
- *Mitigating Bias in AI Algorithms: Ensuring Responsible AI* https://blog.leena.ai/mitigating-bias-in-ai/
- *Library of Content - The Algorithmic Justice League* https://www.ajl.org/library/home
- *Algorithmic transparency and accountability* https://knowledgehub.transparency.org/assets/uploads/kproducts/Algorithmic-Transparency_2021.pdf
- *The EU and U.S. diverge on AI regulation: A transatlantic ...* https://www.brookings.edu/articles/the-eu-and-us-diverge-on-ai-regulation-a-transatlantic-comparison-and-steps-to-alignment/
- *How AI is powering grassroots solutions for communities* https://www.weforum.org/stories/2025/09/how-ai-is-powering-grassroots-solutions-for-community-challenges/
- *NLC AI Advisory Committee* https://www.nlc.org/initiative/nlc-ai-advisory-committee/
- *Real-World Case Studies of Human-AI Collaboration* https://smythos.com/developers/agent-development/human-ai-collaboration-case-studies/
- *Promoting AI for Good in the Global South – Highlights* https://infojustice.org/archives/46490

- *Bridging the Digital Divide: Leveraging AI for Inclusive ...* https://www.usaii.org/ai-insights/bridging-the-digital-divide-leveraging-ai-for-inclusive-transformation-in-rural-communities
- *How Culture Shapes What People Want from AI | Stanford HAI* https://hai.stanford.edu/news/how-culture-shapes-what-people-want-ai
- *6 AI Myths Debunked* https://www.gartner.com/smarterwithgartner/5-ai-myths-debunked
- *Guide to Deepfake Detection* https://www.paravision.ai/whitepaper-a-practical-guide-to-deepfake-detection/
- *The Future Trajectory of Artificial Intelligence and Its Impact on ...* https://www.researchgate.net/publication/392216095_Beyond_Automation_The_Future_Trajectory_of_Artificial_Intelligence_and_Its_Impact_on_Human_Life
- *A Practical Toolkit for Information Literacy in the Age of AI* https://www.oregon.gov/ode/educator-resources/teachingcontent/Documents/Navigating%20Now_%20A%20Practical%20Toolkit%20for%20Information%20Literacy%20in%20the%20Age%20of%20AI.pdf
- *America's AI Action Plan: Scalable AI for States, Cities & ...* https://techsur.solutions/americas-ai-action-plan-part-2-ai-for-the-public-good-what-the-plan-means-for-states-local-governments-and-nonprofits/
- *Algorithmic Justice League - Unmasking AI harms and biases* https://www.ajl.org/
- *Responsible AI for customer service: A checklist ...* https://salesgroup.ai/responsible-ai-for-customer-service/
- *5 Journal Prompts for AI Understanding & Integration* https://journalprompts.net/ai-understanding-prompts

www.ingramcontent.com/pod-product-compliance
Lightning Source LLC
LaVergne TN
LVHW050936210926
848482LV00013B/638
* 9 7 9 8 3 4 8 5 2 0 8 9 2 *